NUTSHEL

CONSUM W
IN A NUTSHELL

Other Titles in the Series

AUSTRALIA
The Law Book Company
Brisbane • Sydney • Melbourne • Perth

CANADA
Carswell
Ottawa • Toronto • Calgary • Montreal • Vancouver

AGENTS
Steimatzky's Agency Ltd., Tel Aviv;
N.M. Tripathi (Private) Ltd., Bombay;
Eastern Law House (Private) Ltd., Calcutta;
M.P.P. House, Bangalore;
Universal Book Traders, Delhi;
Aditya Books, Delhi;
MacMillan Shuppan KK, Tokyo;
Pakistan Law House, Karachi, Lahore

NUTSHELLS

CONSUMER LAW IN A NUTSHELL

by

Sandra Silberstein, LL.B. (HONS.)
Solicitor and Senior Lecturer in Law
Leeds Metropolitan University

London • Sweet & Maxwell • 1994

Published in 1994 by Sweet & Maxwell Limited of
South Quay Plaza, 183 Marsh Wall, London, E14 9FT
Phototypeset by Wyvern Typesetting Limited, Bristol
Printed in England by Clays Ltd., St Ives plc

A CIP Catalogue record for this book is available from the British Library

ISBN 0–421–503602

*To Martin, Daniel,
Rebecca and Deborah
With much love*

CONTENTS

1. CONSUMER TRANSACTIONS GOVERNED BY THE 1979 SALE OF GOODS ACT

Consumer transactions are based on the law of contract. The consumer is agreeing to purchase goods or services and the seller in return agrees to provide them. Therefore all consumer law students must ensure that they understand the basics of contract law before moving onto the special rules and statutes governing consumer law. The major Act which assists consumers is the Sale of Goods Act 1979. This governs all transactions where "goods" are transferred for a monetary consideration called the price.

The word "goods" is defined by section 61 of the 1979 Act, and includes all personal chattels and money and things attached to or forming part of the land which are agreed to be severed before sale.

The consideration has to be monetary consideration (see *Esso Petroleum Co. Ltd.* v. *Customs and Excise Commissioners* 1976) so that if a consumer merely "swaps or exchanges goods" then the transaction cannot be covered by the Sale of Goods Act 1979. (It will in fact be governed by The Supply of Goods and Services Act 1982, see later p. 32.)

However, where the consumer hands in goods in part-exchange and adds cash to make up the balance, then however small the amount of cash, the transaction is governed by the *Sale of Goods Act*. (See *e.g. Aldridge* v. *Johnson* 1857.) Therefore, if Joe Bloggs part exchanges his £4,000 car against a £7,000 one, and adds £3,000 cash the transaction is covered by the Sale of Goods Act.

Once it is established that the transaction is governed by the Act, the following conditions are implied into the contract. Naturally the consumer may well have asked and agreed certain terms about the goods, in which case some matters may well have become express terms of the contract as well as applying the implied conditions. The significance of the fact that there are implied *conditions* will be dealt with later when remedies are considered.

In every contract for the Sale of Goods, section 13 of the 1979 Act states that where there is a sale of goods by description there is an implied condition that the goods will correspond with their description.

What is a sale by description?

(a) 10 rolls of ready pasted vinyl wallpaper from a larger consignment Batch No. 1234.
(b) Sales of specific goods which the buyer has not seen but is relying on the description supplied (see, *e.g. Varley* v. *Whipp*, below).
(c) Sales of specific goods which the buyer has seen if they are sold as goods answering a description, *e.g.* 1992 Ford Escort 10,000 miles.
(d) Sales in Supermarkets where the goods are selected by the buyer.

Section 13 applies to all sales both by private individuals and businesses so all sellers are caught by its provisions.

(See *Varley* v. *Whipp* 1900 – private sale of second-hand reaping machine, described as new the previous year.) This was a sale by description, so the buyer was entitled to reject as the goods did not match their description.

Beale v. *Taylor* 1967

Sale of car described as Herald Convertible, White, 1961.
The buyer inspected the car and purchased it.
In fact the car was two halves welded together, the back of it being a 1200 1961 Herald Convertible, and the front part being an earlier model. The Court of Appeal held that this was a sale by description. The argument was put forward by the seller that the buyer was buying specific goods and had inspected them. This he argued prevented them from being a sale by description. This was rejected by the court. The buyer was entitled to a remedy and was awarded £125. (The price less the scrap value.)

The condition applies to the purchase of all goods selected by the buyer in supermarkets. *See* section 13(3) which states that a sale of goods is not prevented from being a sale by description by reason only that being exposed for sale or hire they are selected by the buyer. Therefore, if the consumer selects goods from the supermarket shelf described as peaches, or 100 per cent. wool sweater, and the tin turns out to contain pears and the sweater to be a wool mixture with acrylic, there has been a breach of this condition. Nowadays as we move into an era where shoppers select their own goods from large stores and hypermarkets without help from sales assistants but relying on signs and packaging, this section assumes a high level of importance. Television shopping channels will also add to its significance.

Reliance

There must be some reliance by the buyer on the words which form part of the description for it to be a sale by description. In a commercial case *Reardon Smith* v. *Hansen Tangen* 1976, the House of Lords held that the mark of identification given to an oil tanker did not form part of the description (it was unimportant and no reliance had been placed on it) and in *Harlingdon & Leinster* v. *Christopher Hull Fine Art* 1991, the Court of Appeal decided that in a transaction between two art dealers, as the buyer had not relied on the description, it was not a sale by description. The seller had attempted to make it clear he was not an expert in a particular field of painting and that the buyer basically bought the painting "at his own risk." It should also be noted this was a highly specialised sale of goods where the buyer could be judged to be more of an expert than the seller, a situation which does not normally arise in the majority of consumer sales.

However, in standard consumer cases the buyer will heavily rely on the description, *e.g.* 100 per cent. wool sweater; 1992 Ford Escort, 10,000 miles; and the problem of it not being a sale by description because of lack of reliance on the description will not normally arise.

Section 13(2) states that if the sale be by sample as well as description it is not sufficient that the bulk of the goods corresponds with the sample, if the goods do not correspond with the description. This is especially useful in furniture sales where consumers are likely to choose from samples. If the carpet is described as 100 per cent. wool, even if the customer is given the same carpet as the sample, if the carpet is not 100 per cent. wool there is a breach of condition.

In Arcos Ltd. v. *Ronaasen* 1933

The goods in question were described as "half inch wooden staves"

Five per cent. of the consignment which was delivered was half an inch thick, many staves were half inch – 9/16", and many more were wider still. Lord Atkin made his famous speech in this case when ordering to such specific quantities:

> "A ton does not mean about a ton, or a yard about a yard. Still less, when you descend to minute measurements, does half an inch mean about half an inch? IF THE SELLER WANTS A MARGIN HE MUST STIPULATE FOR IT." The buyer was therefore entitled to reject as the goods did not match their description.

Thus this case could be extremely useful for the consumer do-it-yourself person, but Lord Atkin's comments must be noted and many retailers stipulate a fairly generous tolerance level nowadays.

Remedies

Section 13 is a condition which means that the buyer is able in terms of a remedy to reject the goods and obtain a refund. Some examples below illustrate how the buyer can benefit from this. Particularly useful in terms of a remedy is section 30 of the Sale of Goods Act 1979 which states what a buyer can do when he ends up with different quantities from what was ordered. Because a different amount has been obtained, there has been a breach of description.

What happens if the seller sends too many of the goods ordered, *e.g.* three pan sets instead of one. The buyer can reject all three sets, or keep the one he ordered and return the other two, or he can keep all three – paying for them at the contract rate (ss.30(2) and (3)).

The buyer is *not* obliged to accept delivery by instalments unless he has agreed. If a lesser amount arrives than that to which he agreed, he can reject them or keep them, paying a proportion of the contract rate. So that if three pan sets have been ordered and only one arrives, the buyer can keep that one or reject it.

If the buyer receives the goods ordered mixed with goods of a different description, then the buyer can reject all the goods or reject the goods not answering the description. He has no statutory right to keep the mixed goods, so if the pan set arrives with a dinner service the whole lot can be rejected or the pan set kept. *Note*: There is no right to acquire the dinner service (s.30(4)).

Re Moore v. Landauer 1921 2 K.B. 519.

Here, instead of pan sets, the goods were a consignment of fruit, ordered in boxes of 30 tins. When delivered, some boxes contained 24 tins, some contained 30 – although the correct number of tins was present. The court held that this was mixed goods as the order was for boxes of 30 tins and therefore the buyer was entitled to reject the whole consignment.

In cases where a breach of description is involved, students ought to always consider the possibility of a misrepresentation arising. Also to be discussed later is possible criminal liability for the retailer under the Trade Descriptions Act 1968.

2. LIABILITY FOR DEFECTIVE GOODS

The major problem facing consumers is that the goods they have purchased turn out to be defective: the cooker breaks down after a month; the television set blows up; the sweater shrinks to half its size after being washed correctly.

What assistance does the 1979 Act afford consumers?

Section 14 starts where goods are sold *in the course of a business*, so it only covers the situation when the retailer is in business. It does not cover private sales. However, it should be noted the status of the buyer is irrelevant. Section 14 applies to business buyers as well as to private buyers.

For consumers, the phrase "in the course of a business" normally presents few problems. Sales by stores, garages or mail order are obviously made in the course of a business and it makes no difference that the seller was handling a particular kind of product for the first time.

The Act in section 61 says that "in the course of a business" includes a profession and the activities of a local authority, government or department. The words have been discussed recently in relation to:

(a) Unfair Contract Terms Act 1977 (see *R.* v. *B. Customs Brokers Ltd.* v. *U.D.T.* 1988);
(b) The Trade Descriptions Act 1968 (see *Devlin* v. *Hall* 1990 and *Davies* v. *Sumner* 1984).

It must be noted that the argument in (a) concerned exclusion clauses and if the buyer in this case would have been deemed to have acted "in the course of a business" he would probably have been bound by a harsh exclusion clause. The Court of Appeal therefore, in its judgment, generally not liking exclusion clauses, said that for the buyer to be acting in the course of a business where the activity was merely incidental, a degree of regularity had to be established before it could be said that the activity was an *integral* part of the business and so carried on in the course of that business. In this case, the car was purchased by a Limited Company, whose main business was moving freight, to be used by the Managing Director. There was no regular practice of buying and selling cars and the court said it was a mere incidental activity and therefore, because no regularity had been established, it was not done in the course of a business. The same view has been taken in the two cases under the Trade Descriptions Act, but students are asked to note once again that this is a criminal statute and the defendants would have been subject to fines or imprisonment if they would have been held to have been acting in the course of a business.

As yet the phrase has not been judicially considered at the higher levels in relation to section 14 so guidance can only be gleaned from the above cases.

Merchantable quality

Assuming that the seller is acting in the course of a business, section 14 says there is a condition that the goods are of merchantable quality.

An attempt to define merchantable quality is made in section 14(6) – this says goods of any kind are of merchantable quality if they are as fit for the purpose or purposes for which goods of that kind are commonly bought as it is reasonable to expect, having regard to any description applied to them, the price if relevant, and all the other relevant circumstances and according to *Rogers* v. *Parish (Scarborough) Ltd.* 1987 this is all that needs to be considered, the older cases do not need to be looked at when considering the statutory definition (*per* Lord Muskill).

Below are some of the problems facing consumers in respect of defective goods:

(a) What if they work but are dented and scratched?
(b) What happens if the new goods can be easily repaired?
(c) How does the section apply (if at all) to second-hand goods?
(d) What about the effect of manufacturers' guarantees?

The section will now be studied in detail to answer these questions, amongst others.

As far as most consumers are concerned, if they pay a higher price they expect better quality and, as *section 14(6)* states: price is a factor to be taken into consideration when deciding whether goods are of merchantable quality or not. The case of *Brown* v. *Craiks* 1970 supports this view, *i.e.* the more the consumer pays, the higher his quality expectations are.

What about new goods? How long do we expect them to last for? Several car cases decided in recent years try to throw light on this particular question.

In *Bernstein* v. *Pamson Motors* 1987, a new Nissan car was purchased for cash by Mr. Bernstein. After three weeks and some 140 miles he was driving his car along the motorway when the engine "seized up." The reason for this was that a drop of sealant, which had got into the lubrication system when the car was being assembled, had caused a blockage which deprived the car of oil. In spite of a controversial judgment on other matters, Rougier J. held, applying section 14(6) that the car was not of merchantable quality. A consumer who purchases a new car is entitled to expect that the engine will not seize up after three weeks.

What about appearance defects on new cars? In *Rogers* v. *Parish* 1987, a new Range Rover car was purchased under a conditional sale agreement. On delivery there were defects in the engine, gearbox and bodywork and the oil seals were unsound. The plaintiff drove the car for some six months, constantly complained, but managed between visits to the garage to clock up 5,500 miles. At the end of six months faults still remained in the gearbox, engine and bodywork.

On the question of the bodywork defects and the class of comfort to be expected interior wise from a new car; the Court of Appeal said categorically that appearance defects in a new car can, depending on the price and standard expected, render a car to be of unmerchantable quality. There have been calls for an amendment in section 14(6) to take this specifically into account and it is hoped in the near future that a new definition will emerge giving more emphasis to this appearance point.

The Court of Appeal decided in this case again that the car was not of merchantable quality and specifically tried to answer three questions:

(a) If the defect was able to be repaired, did this mean that the car was of merchantable quality? The answer given to this was no, so that if a consumer buys goods which would work perfectly if they were repaired, do they have to accept a repair? Clearly the answer is no, particularly where the defect occurs very soon after purchase, but as will be seen later, from a practical point of view sometimes a repair is the only option open, as the consumer may be unwilling to take the matter further.

(b) What about the effect of a manufacturer's warranty? If a consumer buys goods knowing that if they are defective they will be repaired free of charge under warranty, should the consumer anticipate defects and therefore the expectation of merchantable quality is lower. This argument was rejected. It was stated very sensibly that a warranty could only increase expectations, it certainly could not diminish them.

(c) The third argument, that the car could be driven, albeit intermittently between visits to the garage, was also rejected. The
buyer had purchased a car for comfort, transportation and
reliability. He was entitled to this constantly and not
intermittently!

As far as consumers are concerned, most of the cases which are
litigated tend to involve cars – being the most expensive product
consumers usually purchase. Everyday items such as toasters,
clothes, etc., are either litigated through the Small Claims Court
(see later) and the decisions are largely unreported, or else the consumer unfortunately decides the time and irritation involved are not
worth it.

WHAT ABOUT SECOND-HAND GOODS?

Does the condition apply? The answer is Yes, but obviously age
and price are to be taken into account and the reasonable buyer's
expectations. In *Bartlett* v. *Sidney Marcus* 1965 the plaintiff purchased
a second-hand Jaguar for £950. He was told the clutch needed a
small repair. However, when the car had been driven for 300 miles
the car required a complete new clutch, costing £84. *Held*: the car
was of merchantable quality, a clutch defect is the kind that could
be anticipated on a second hand car. The point about Mr. Bartlett
knowing about the clutch will be discussed later.

In *Crowther* v. *Shannon Motor Co.* 1975 again the car involved was
a second-hand Jaguar purchased for £390. This time the car, which
had travelled 82,000 miles, was driven a further 2,500 miles in three
weeks when the engine seized up. The Court of Appeal said this
was a defect which could not reasonably be expected from a car of
this age and mileage and there was a breach of section 14(2).

In *Business Application Specialists* v. *Nationwide Credit* 1988 the
second-hand car in question, a Mercedes, was purchased on hire
purchase terms. The price was £14,850. After being driven for 800
miles the car broke down, suffering from loss of compression. The
defect was likened to the clutch one in *Bartlett* v. *Sidney Marcus* 1965
and the car was deemed to be of merchantable quality.

In *Shine* v. *General Guarantee* 1988, the car was a second hand Fiat
X19, purchased on hire purchase terms for £4,400. The car had in
fact been written off and disposed of for salvage purposes. The
plaintiff discovered this after three months and sought to reject it.
On the question of whether the car was of merchantable quality,
the Court of Appeal said it was valid to take the buyer's expectations
into account and ask what did the buyer think he was getting and
what did he actually get?

As Bush J. said, what was the plaintiff entitled to think he was buying? – He thought he was buying an enthusiast's car, a car of the mileage shown and at the sort of price cars of that age and condition could be expected to fetch. What he in fact was buying was a car which had been submerged in water for at least 24 hours, and which was an insurance company write off. He was buying potentially a rogue car and irrespective of its condition, it was in fact one which no member of the public, knowing the facts, would touch with a barge pole unless they could get it at "a substantially reduced price to reflect the risk they were taking." The car was not of merchantable quality.

Defects drawn to buyer's attention

Section 14(2)(a) says that goods must be of merchantable quality unless the defect has been specifically drawn to the buyer's attention before the contract is made. Section 14(2)(b) says where the buyer has examined the goods there is no condition as to merchantable quality as regards defects which that examination ought to have revealed. It is therefore better to advise buyers not to examine goods before purchase. The buyer of a sweater with an obvious hole might fall within this exception if he examined the goods before purchase and missed the hole. See also *Bartlett* v. *Sidney Marcus* 1965.

In *R. & B. Customs Brokers Ltd.* v. *U.D.T.* 1988 the purchaser was aware of the fact his second-hand Colt Shogun had a leaky roof before the contract was concluded. (This was because the sale was made on a conditional sale agreement. The plaintiff managing director was allowed to take the car away before the Finance Company accepted him and therefore concluded the contract. For the mechanics of a conditional sale agreement, see p. 16, below.) This defect could never be repaired. The Court of Appeal ruled there was no breach of section 14(2) as to merchantable quality because the plaintiff knew of the defect.

Section 14 applies to *all* goods supplied under the contract so that if an extra is added, *e.g.* as in *Wilson* v. *Rickett Cockerell* 1954 (detonator in a bag of coalite) the defendant cannot argue he supplied the goods and a detonator. The effect of the total package was to render the coalite unmerchantable.

Section 14 creates "strict liability," *i.e.* it does not matter how careful the defendant is in checking his stock, if he sells defective goods he is liable. *Frost* v. *Aylesbury Dairy* 1905.

Remember as well, section 14 creates contractual liability, it is the retailer who is liable under section 14 to the buyer. If the retailer chooses to join another party into the proceedings then he can do so but he remains the one who is primarily liable. This is why it is

vital from a retailer's point of view to have good indemnity clauses,
reputable suppliers and good insurance cover.

---

3. FITNESS FOR PURPOSE

Section 14(3) says that where the seller in the course of a business,
expressly or by implication makes known any particular purpose for
which the goods are being bought, there is an implied *condition* that
the goods supplied are reasonably fit for that purpose except where
the circumstances show that the buyer does not rely, or that it is
unreasonable for him to rely on the *skill or judgment of the seller*.

As consumers we frequently buy goods that only have one purpose. If a washing machine is purchased or a hot water bottle, then
the buyer does not usually ask the sales assistant whether the
machine will wash clothes or whether the bottle will keep them
warm. The purpose is implied because they are one purpose goods.
Therefore, if the goods are defective there is a breach of section 14(2)
and section 14(3) (*Priest* v. *Last* 1903 (hole in hot water bottle)). In
the case of choosing goods, the consumer if he goes to a reputable
store is entitled to assume that the seller has chosen his stock "using
his skill" and therefore the requirement in section 14(3) is satisfied
(*Grant* v. *Australian Knitting Mills* 1936).

Supposing the buyer wishes to purchase a printer to accompany
his computer. He visits a reputable store and asks for printer XZ
2000, not mentioning anything else to the retailer. It turns out that
this printer is incompatible with his particular computer, but will
work with many other brands. There is no breach of section 14(2)
and no breach of section 14(3) as the buyer has not relied on the
skill and judgment of the seller. When buying multi-purpose goods
such as these buyers should always be advised to ask as many questions as possible to get the maximum benefit under section 14(3).
This was the case in *Griffiths* v. *Peter Conway Ltd.* 1939 where the
buyer's skin was irritated by a fur coat purchased from the defendant. This would not have affected most buyers. There was no breach
of section 14(2) or section 14(3) as the fact the buyer had abnor-
mally sensitive skin was never communicated to the seller.

In *R. & B. Customs Brokers Ltd.* v. *UDT* 1988 (see earlier) the car
had a leaky roof. There was no breach of merchantable quality

because of the proviso to section 14 that the buyer was aware of the defect. However, whenever it rained the car was impossible to use. When the buyer purchased the car he did not say to the salesman "I want to drive it in England and it rains in England. Will I be dry?" The car was not fit for its purpose of being driven in England and there was a breach of section 14(3).

The effect of the word condition

It has been seen so far that the terms in sections 13, 14(2) and (3) are all conditions. Their importance insofar as buyers are concerned is in relation to the remedies they can pursue. If there is a breach of condition, the buyer is entitled to reject the goods, recover any monies paid and is entitled to any further damages resulting as a natural and probable consequence of the breach.

This is of course the rule for remoteness of damage in the case of *Hadley* v. *Baxendale* 1854.

Remedies for breach of contract in Sale of Goods Contracts

As stated above, sections 13 and 14 are conditions normally entitling the buyer to reject the goods, however section 11(4) of the Sale of Goods Act states "where a contract of sale is not severable and the buyer has *accepted* the goods the breach of any condition is to be treated as a breach of warranty." The remedy for a breach of warranty is damages therefore it is vital to know if acceptance has occurred for this can greatly affect the remedy.

What is acceptance?

This is governed by sections 34 and 35 of the Act and it is section 35 which will be of most relevance to consumers. Section 35 says acceptance can occur in three ways:

(a) by intimation – so beware the implications of signing delivery notes on packaged goods without putting "not inspected";
(b) act after delivery inconsistent with the seller's ownership. This is much more important in commercial rather than consumer cases;
(c) by the buyer retaining the goods beyond a reasonable time. If the buyer keeps the goods beyond a reasonable time he is deemed to have accepted them and is entitled to damages only.

The questions to be asked therefore are:

(a) When does the time start to run?
(b) What is considered reasonable?

Time starts to run from when the goods were delivered to the buyer *not* from when he became aware of the defect. What is reasonable is a question of fact in every case. Unfortunately there is very little consumer case law on the point other than the High Court decision in *Bernstein* v. *Pamson Motors* 1987 where it will be recalled Mr. Bernstein had his car for three weeks when the engine seized up. The first time Mr. Bernstein knew anything was wrong was when his car blew up on the motorway. He was offered a replacement engine but wanted a new car or a refund. Rougier J. held, as stated earlier, that there was a breach of merchantable quality but that by "keeping" the car for three weeks Mr. Bernstein had accepted the car and was entitled therefore to damages only, which meant in his case a replacement engine. Clearly this case is most unsatisfactory as far as consumers are concerned for it is difficult to see what else Mr. Bernstein could have done. The case was "backed" by several consumer organisations, including the AA, but before the Court of Appeal could judge further it was reported that a settlement had been reached with Mr. Bernstein. This is unfortunate as the High Court decision remains reported, but it is only High Court and is therefore of limited authority. Unfortunately it is a case that has been seized upon with relish by retailers as can be imagined!

The Consumers Association and the National Consumer Council are pressing vigorously for statutory reforms in this area but to date no legislation has yet come onto the statute books.

However, one important step forward has been taken by several leading car manufacturers, notably Ford, Rover and Vauxhall, who have all come out in June 1993 with varying promises to exchange or refund money. Rover's commitment, for instance, promises that "If for any reason you are not completely satisfied with your new Rover car, you can return it within 30 days or 1000 miles whichever comes first, for an exchange or full refund." Ford offers to exchange or refund within 12 months if a persistent fault cannot be cured.

> "in the unlikely event you experience a persistent problem and we cannot fix it after *3* attempts or your vehicle is off the road due to manufacturing defects for 30 days or more (while undergoing or awaiting defect rectification by authorised Ford dealers) we will replace it or provide a refund – without charge if your vehicle is less than 6 months old. After 6 months the customer will be expected to make a contribution to the costs based on published RAC rates per mile for the description and to interest if a finance agreement is applicable."

This move has been warmly welcomed by Consumer Associations. The so-called Lemon Laws in America and the failure of the Consumer Guarantees Bill to reach the statute book (this would have given consumers more protection in the event of persistent unrepair-able faults) caused great consternation in that consumers in this country were being treated less favourably than their counterparts abroad. So far Jaguar, who have operated a similar return scheme in America, have received only 1 per cent. of their cars back accord-ing to their Customer Relations Department.

Problems on acceptance do not arise in hire purchase contracts or conditional sale agreements. This will be discussed further later. See p. 16.

The measure of damages

Therefore, if the buyer has not accepted the goods he will be entitled to reject. If he has accepted then damages only is the remedy.

As a Sale of Goods Act transaction is only a contract then, as stated earlier, the rules for the payment of damages are based on the case of *Hadley* v. *Baxendale* 1854. Sections 51–53 of the Sale of Goods Act sets out in more detail the kind of damages that can be claimed and how a figure can be reached, but it is important that students remember that what they are considering is the rule in *Hadley* v. *Baxendale* 1854.

For example, suppose George purchases a kettle. After two weeks the kettle explodes, injuring George who is standing nearby, and ruining George's floorcovering and kitchen units. George is entitled under the Sale of Goods Act to claim a breach of section 14 as to merchantable quality. Assuming that he has not accepted the goods, he can claim a refund for the product from the retailer. As his personal injuries and property damage resulted from the breach he is entitled to claim damages for these losses based on the rule in *Hadley* v. *Baxendale* 1854.

For the next example let us suppose George purchased a music system six months ago which has "chewed up" four cassettes costing £30. Because of the time factor George will almost certainly have accepted the goods and will be unable to reject. He will be entitled to damages for breach of warranty for the product (s.53). In this case it will be the cost of putting the unit right. He will also be entitled to claim the cost of the four cassettes under the rule in *Hadley* v. *Baxendale* 1854.

Other damages issues

Other issues facing consumers who have purchased defective goods are:

   (a) Even if they can obtain a refund they may have to pay more for the same goods elsewhere. These additional costs arise as a result of the natural and probable consequences of the breach and can be reclaimed.

(b) The seller is unable to deliver the goods on time.

Suppose George orders a bed for £300 with delivery to take place on Friday. If the bed is not delivered George has suffered a breach of contract but unless he made "time of the essence" he is not entitled to regard the contract as "terminated (*Rickards* v. *Oppenheim* 1950)". He is entitled to damages (if he can prove loss) but will have to give the retailer another chance to deliver. If the retailer fails to deliver this time George can terminate. If George is put to extra costs buying the goods elsewhere he can claim these additional costs.

It should be noted that there is *no* replacement remedy provided in the Sale of Goods Act.

The only remedies available under the statute are to reject the goods which would give rise to a refund plus damages where appropriate, or a damages only remedy.

However, as far as most consumers are concerned, if they acquire replacement new goods they would be perfectly happy and from a practical point of view this is what is negotiated in many cases. Again it must be noted from a practical point of view that if a consumer purchases goods which are defective, a large number of retailers will, for instance in the case of a major domestic appliance, *e.g.* freezer, washing machine, offer to repair in the first instance, rather than refund or exchange.

Although we have seen that legally the buyer could be entitled to reject because of a breach of merchantable quality, the vast majority of buyers will "accept" the repair as they do not wish to pursue court action. If advice is sought in a case like this, advise the buyer to make it clear that by agreeing to the repair he is not "accepting" the goods and should the fault occur again within a short period of time he will be entitled to all his remedies under the Sale of Goods Act.

The replacement remedy is one for which many consumer groups and retail organisations are currently lobbying.

Damages for distress and disappointment

This is a head of damages which should not be overlooked in consumer cases despite the reluctance of the Court of Appeal in the case of *Hayes* v. *Dodd* 1990 to extend the ambit of this kind of award. Damages for distress have been awarded in holiday cases, for loss of photographs, and in one instance where the bride's wedding carriage failed to turn up. ((1988) New L.J. 906).

Most of these examples involve services consumer contracts and will be discussed later.

---

4. OTHER CONSUMER TRANSACTIONS

In the previous chapters transactions covered by the Sale of Goods Act have been considered. However, there are many transactions consumer buyers make and, because there is no "transfer of property for a monetary consideration called the price" the transaction is not governed by the Sale of Goods Act.

It has been seen that if Ben buys a car for cash, then if the car turns out to be defective, Ben has a remedy under the Sale of Goods Act.

Suppose:

> Ben decided to buy his car on hire purchase terms (the mechanics of this are discussed later). In this case there is merely a "bailment of goods." The Finance Company owns the goods until the final instalment is paid so there is no transfer of property. The car is defective. What can Ben do?

This hire purchase consumer transaction is governed by Supply of Goods (Implied Terms) Act 1973. Sections 9 & 10 of this Act mirror exactly the provisions of sections 13 and 14 of the Sale of Goods Act (a great sigh of relief from all students and practitioners at this point as there are no new provisions to be learnt) so that if the car is defective there will be a breach of section 10 of the Act as to merchantable quality and fitness for purpose. All the student has to realise is that where a hire purchase transaction is involved, section 10 of the 1973 Act must be looked at instead of section 14 of the 1979 Act.

Differences in Approach

There is however one major difference between hire purchase defective goods transactions and straight sale of goods transactions and this involves the issue of acceptance. Students will recall that Sale of Goods transactions are caught by section 11(4) of the Sale of Goods Act which has the effect of turning a condition into a warranty if acceptance has occurred. There is no equivalent provi-

sion in the 1973 Act so no issue of acceptance arises, only the
common law doctrine of affirmation.

Affirmation v. Acceptance

Basically acceptance occurs whether or not the consumer knew
of the defect and time starts to run from the moment of delivery.
Affirmation on the other hand can only occur when the defect is
known and time starts to run from that point. It can be seen from
a consumer's point of view that this is a more favourable doctrine.
In *Shine* v. *General Guarantee* 1988 a hire purchase transaction, it was
held that by his actions the buyer had affirmed the contract (he had
been slow to reject the goods). Therefore he was entitled to damages
only.

However, in *Farnworth Finance Facilities* v. *Attryde* 1970, the goods
in question were a motor bike. Some four months and 400 miles
later, Mr. Attryde attempted to reject the goods. *Held*: entitled to
do so. As Lord Denning said: "A man only affirms a contract when
he knows of the defects and by his conduct elects to go on with the
contract despite them." Again in *Yeoman Credit* v. *Apps* 1962 the
buyer had the use of the motor bike for some time and was entitled
to reject it and recover nearly all monies paid. A small allowance
for use was made.

Conditional Sale Transactions

This type of credit transaction is covered by the Sale of Goods
Act as is a sale subject to a condition. However, in The Supply of
Goods (Implied Terms) Act 1973 it is enacted that section 11(4)
does not apply to these transactions. The doctrine of acceptance
does not apply again, only affirmation.

In *Rogers* v. *Parish (Scarborough)* 1987 the buyer of a new Range
Rover under a conditional sale agreement had the goods for six
months, doing 5,000 miles with constant complaints and return
visits to the garage. *Held*: he had not affirmed the contract and was
entitled to a refund.

Hire Transactions

These are governed by The Supply of Goods and Services Act
1982. Sections 8 and 9 are the equivalents of sections 13 and 14 of
the Sale of Goods Act, so that if Ben hires a car and it is defective,
he has to seek a remedy under this statute.

Exchange Transactions

If there is a pure exchange transaction, involving no extra cash
then there is no monetary consideration, (see *Esso Petroleum* v.

Customs and Excise Commissioners 1976 – World Cup coins 1966 promotion, consideration was not cash but buying of four gallons of petrol) therefore the transaction is not governed by the Sale of Goods and Services Act. Therefore if Ben swaps his Mercedes for a Mini the transaction is not governed by the Sale of Goods Act but is instead again governed by Part I of the Supply of Goods and Services Act. This time sections 3 and 4 apply. These are the equivalents of sections 13 and 14 of the Sale of Goods Act. Again the doctrine of affirmation applies.

If, however, any additional cash is paid over with the exchange goods, then the transaction is back under the Sale of Goods Act. Therefore, if Ben hands over his car together with £1,000 to acquire his new one, the Sale of Goods Act governs the transaction.

The materials part of a work and materials contract

Ben takes his car to be serviced. As a consumer he is paying for the work to be completed to his satisfaction but the supplier will also be using parts in the course of the services. It is liability for those parts, in the event that they are defective, or do not match their description, which is now being considered.

Liability for parts supplied under a work and materials contract is governed again by sections 3 and 4 of Part I of the Supply of Goods and Services Act (the equivalents of sections 13 and 14). Again the doctrine of affirmation applies. Therefore, if Ben's car is supposed to be fitted with genuine "Vord" parts and fake "Boda" parts have been used, Ben will use this statute to pursue his action.

The service part of a work and materials contract and pure service contracts

In the example given above, of Ben taking his car to have it serviced, it is the service part of the contract which is now being considered.

In every work and materials contract and every pure service contract there is an implied term under section 13 of the Supply of Goods and Services Act that the work will be carried out with reasonable care and skill. Notice the difference between liability for failure to perform the work properly. The work has to be carried out with *reasonable* care and skill. The standard by which this can be judged is therefore an *objective negligence* based standard as set in the famous case of *Bolam* v. *Friern Hospital* 1957, a case involving the medical profession whereby to decide whether a doctor is liable for negligence, he must be compared with the average doctor in the profession.

Ben therefore would have to show if he is complaining about the work that the average garage would have performed the work differently. This is the case in all matters involving services, whether it is a garage, a decorator or a plumber, for example, where the quality of the services rendered is claimed to be unsatisfactory.

Two other terms are implied into service contracts. By section 14 where *no* time has been agreed for performing the contract, the supplier must perform it within a reasonable time.

By section 15 where *no* price has been agreed, then a reasonable price must be charged. If the supplier has quoted a very high price and this has been accepted by the consumer, then section 15 will not help him. He has entered into a bad bargain.

Remedies for breach of services contracts

The normal remedy for a breach of services contract is damages to put the poor work right and to restore the aggrieved consumer into the position he would have been in, had the contract been performed properly.

Damages for distress, disappointment and inconvenience have been frequently awarded for breach of services contracts despite the restrictive approach in *Hayes* v. *Dodd* 1990. Holidays are a particular area which remain unaffected by this decision, *e.g. Jarvis* v. *Swan Tours* 1973 as are "lost" photographs, *e.g. Woodman* v. *Photo Trade Processing* 1981.

5. PRODUCT LIABILITY

It has already been noted in Chapter 3 that where a buyer of goods is injured as a result of the product being defective then he can recover for his personal injuries by "latching" them onto a claim that the goods are not of merchantable quality and that the natural and probable consequence of that breach is that an injury occurred, *i.e.* the normal contractual rule for damages as set out in *Hadley* v. *Baxendale* 1854.

This remedy is satisfactory of course, provided the person has actually purchased the goods and therefore has a contract under the Sale of Goods Act or that the supplier is still in existence. However, what happens if the person injured was given the defective product or is a third party injured by it? Prior to 1987 such a person would have had to pursue any claim for personal injury damages using the tort of negligence and the case of *Donoghue* v. *Stevenson* 1932. The difficulties of proving fault, even though a duty of care is owed to the ultimate consumer, meant the consumer faced an uphill battle at times (*Daniels & Daniels* v. *R. White & Sons & Tarbard* 1938).

Faced with these difficulties, and in an attempt to standardise product liability throughout Europe, the Consumer Protection Act 1987 reached the statute books.

Firstly, some general points to notice:

(a) The term product liability means that the person injured by defective products may have the right to sue for damages. Product liability is the term given to laws affecting those rights.

(b) The rights set out earlier under the Sale of Goods Act and in the tort of negligence are in addition to the rights given out in the Consumer Protection Act. The Act does not affect any existing civil laws governing product liability.

(c) The Act implements the European Communities Directive on Product Liability (85/364/EEC)/ dated July 25, 1985.

(d) The Act is *not* retrospective. It only affects products first supplied after March 1, 1988.

THE AIMS OF THE ACT

The major aims of the Act are to impose *strict liability* for defective products, principally on someone who is deemed to be a producer of the product, thus removing the requirement of having to prove fault. The Act seeks to provide a clear route by which an injured person can reach the person responsible for the damage.

Basic Position

It should be noted at the outset that the Act only comes into play where the consumer has a defective product which causes damage. A product which fails to please or does not work properly will have to be dealt with under the Sale of Goods Act, not under the Consumer Protection Act.

Section 2(1) of the Act says where any damage is caused wholly or partly by a defect in a product, every person to whom subsection (2) applies shall be liable for the damage. Therefore, the essential requirements are:

(a) a product;
(b) damage;
(c) defective (in the way of being unsafe);
(d) causation;
(e) Who is liable?

As can be seen there is no fault-based requirement. The Act is aimed at the person who was responsible for the product, not the person who supplied it. Therefore the first consideration is who is liable? Section 2(2) says the following persons are primarily liable:

(a) the producer, *i.e.* the manufacturer;
(b) an own brander who has held himself out as a producer;
(c) the first importer into the European Community.

The main purpose is to provide a clear route for the injured person to sue. Strict liability will attach to anyone who presents themselves as a producer, *e.g.* Sony, Philips, Hoover or to anyone who is an own brander who has held himself out to be a producer of the product, *e.g.* Tesco, Marks & Spencer, Asda; it remains to be seen through case law whether a phrase like "produced for Tesco" will be judged to mean that Tesco are not liable under section 2(2) or whether they will only escape liability by actually naming the manufacturer, *i.e.* "made for J Sainsbury by Fred Bloggs & Co."

The first importer into the European Community is also primarily liable so that if a Japanese television set is imported into France then transported to England where it causes damage to an individual, then the French importer is liable but not the British importer under the Act.

Only in relatively few cases will the supplier be liable. This is where the producer cannot be identified and the supplier is unable to identify anyone further up the chain of supply within a reasonable period of time. Suppliers of products must therefore ensure they keep records of all companies who supply them with goods so that if a claim is made they will be able to pass the injured person on. Even if their supplier has gone into liquidation, the person who actually supplied the goods will have fulfilled their obligations under the Consumer Protection Act by giving a name.

(*Note*: however, if the person actually bought the goods there would be liability under the Sale of Goods Act by virtue of the contractual situation and no escape for the supplier.)

It should be further noted that some products are comprised of a number of different component items. In that case, the manufacturer of the total finished product is liable, *e.g.* a car manufacturer such as Ford, as is the manufacturer of the defective component concerned; *e.g.* if it is a tyre then the tyre manufacturer. The injured person can sue either manufacturer or both, as liability is joint and several. So, if a person is injured in circumstances as outlined above, both Ford and, for example the manufacturers of Dunlop tyres could be drawn into an action.

What is a product?

By section 1(2) a product includes goods or electricity and this is further expanded by the definition in section 45 which states that goods include growing crops and things comprised in land by virtue of being attached to it and any ship, aircraft or vehicle. It is extremely unlikely in the context of an examination question that a problem will be set where the student has to worry about whether the product is covered by the product definition under the Act.

Only one exception should be noted, *i.e.* that unprocessed agricultural products are excluded. They only become a product for the purposes of the Act once they have undergone an industrial process. Various debates took place on this in the House of Lords and are of course reported in *Hansard*. As a result of cases like *Pepper* v. *Hart* 1992 where *Hansard* was referred to in the course of judgments, there is no doubt that when cases are reported under the Act, reference will be made to *Hansard*.

Thus, a farmer who produces contaminated lettuces is not liable to the ultimate consumer under the Act (but could be liable in negligence or in contract) but a processed pea manufacturer would be liable. (*Note*: the defect does *not* have to arise as a result of the industrial process. All it means is that the vegetable or fruit becomes a product and the manufacturer is liable for *any* defect in it.)

What is a defective product?

This is governed by section 3 which states that a defective product is defined as one where the *safety* of the product is not such as persons generally are entitled to expect. A product will not be considered defective simply because it is of poor quality or because a safer version is subsequently put on the market. Defects are likely to fall into three areas:

(a) *Manufacturing*: these should be the easiest to deal with in practice, *e.g.* the hot water bottle which splits because defective rubber has been used.
(b) *Design*: this is going to present more difficulties in practice.
(c) *Misleading Warning Notices*: which fail to advise the consumer

how to use the product properly, or no warning notices at all where a court might feel that a warning should have been given. There are, for example, product liability cases in America where no warnings were placed on a bottle of perfume. When the user stood up in front of a fire and caught fire herself, she argued that a warning should have been placed on the bottle pointing out its inflammability and telling the user not to stand in front of fires. This led to a successful claim.

On a question of causation, the plaintiff must show that the defect caused the damage. Cases in tort, such as *Wilsher* v. *Essex Area Health Authority* 1986, *Kay* v. *Ayreshire* 1982 will no doubt be used in this area where difficult cases arise.

What sort of damage is covered?

It is important to note that only certain kinds of damage are covered by the Act and therefore at the outset, if the kind of damage which does occur is not within section 5 of the Act, it is pointless pursuing a claim and redress under the Sale of Goods Act or negligence must be sought.

A person can sue under the Act (section 5) for:

(a) death;
(b) personal injury;
(c) damage to private property valued above £275.

There is no liability for damage to the product itself or for the loss of, or any damage to, the whole or any part of any product which has been supplied with the product. Thus, if Fred buys a new car and one of the tyres is defective due to a manufacturing defect and Fred has a crash in the car, causing personal injuries and the car is considered to be a "write off," Fred can sue for his personal injury under the Act but cannot sue for the car. He *cannot* argue that the tyre and the chassis are different products thus the tyre has caused damage to other property (as was tried in *Aswan Engineering Establishment Co.* v. *Lupdine Ltd.* 1987). The car was acquired *at one time*, thus any compensation must be achieved via the Sale of Goods Act or negligence. If Fred however replaced the tyres on his car, and the new tyres were defective, this time he *could* claim compensation for his injuries *and* his car because one product, the tyre, caused damage to another product, the car. This of course assumes the car is private property.

Section 5(3) attempts to define private property by saying:

A person shall not be liable under section 2 for damage to property which is not

(a) of a description property ordinarily intended for private use, occupation or consumption; and

(b) intended by the person suffering the loss mainly for his own private use, occupation or consumption. It will be a question of fact whether the property is private and difficulties will arise in "office equipment at home" and "personal items in the office." *Remember*: the property damage must be valued at more than £275. This is to discourage frivolous claims under the Act.

Defences

Even if a manufacturer is liable so far under the Act, the Act creates strict liability *not* absolute liability and in the United Kingdom we have opted to give manufacturers six defences. The burden of proof rests on the defendant.

The defences are:

1. The defect was caused by complying with the law. The defence is only available where the standard is a mandatory one. It will not help a producer where compliance with a standard is only advisory, as is the case with many products conforming to British Standard. The producer must show that the defect was the inevitable consequence of complying with the standard. Needless to say this is unlikely to prove to be a much used defence in practice!

2. That he did not supply the product – this covers cases for instance of theft. A further definition of the word "supply" can be found in section 46.

3. That the supplier is not in business. The aim behind the Act is to impose strict liability on commercial producers and it was never the intention to impose liability on private individuals. However, section 4(1)(c) is worded in such a way that private individuals may be caught, it says:

(a) that the only supply of the product to another by the person proceeded against was otherwise than in the course of a business (so sales of second hand goods by private individuals are not caught by the Act)

and

(b) that the supplier is not a producer (the second-hand situation referred to above). If he is a producer and he did make the goods with a view to profit, then he will be caught by the Act.

Thus, a grandfather who makes a toy for his grandson is a producer but is not doing it with a view to profit so is not caught by the Act. A housewife who makes home-made jam for a local church charity bazaar should not be liable. But, a housewife on a busy coastal route who sells her home-made strawberry jam to passers-by from her front garden would be liable.

4. That the defect did not exist in the product at the time it was supplied by the producer to another. Recent examples involving the spiking of baby food serve to illustrate the point. If the food left the factory in perfect condition and the contamination took place in the supermarket, the manufacturer would not be liable. If the contamination occurred in the factory, the manufacturer would be liable. Of course, if the contamination took place in the supermarket the retailer would incur liability under the Sale of Goods Act for a breach of section 14 of the Sale of Goods Act.

5. The state of scientific and technical knowledge at the relevant time was not such that a producer of products of the same description as the product in question might be expected to have discovered.

This is the most controversial defence provided in the Act, "the state of the art defence." It has been condemned by many commentators as giving producers a "get out" under the Act and in many cases where the Act could have proved to be most useful, *e.g.* in the thalidomide drug case, the manufacturer may still escape liability.

Currently the United Kingdom is involved in proceedings before the European Court as a result of this defence being included in the Act (the U.K. had an option as to whether or not to include the defence). The result of these proceedings could affect matters in the future but at the moment the defence is included in the Statute until 1997.

In order to avail themselves of the defence, producers will have to show that at the relevant time they could not have been expected to discover the defect. In the House of Lords debate, Vol. 483, No. 25, col. 841, it was said:

> "It will be of no help to the producer to plead how difficult or how expensive it had or might have been to have found the answers to that defect. If other producers of products of that type had the knowledge available to them, then the defence is of no use to the producer of the product."

The test under the Act is an objective one, not what the actual defendant knew, but what was actually known at the time. Again, due to lack of case law, it remains to be seen how this provision will work in practice.

6. That a producer of a component produced a defective product and the defect was wholly attributable to instructions he had been given by the principal producer. This is a defence only open to a component manufacturer who has produced goods to a certain specification and the principal product is defective. The component manufacturer may be able to escape liability although the principal manufacturer could not. Thus if Bloggs Ltd. supplies a component to Classit Ltd. and the component makes the product defective because Classit's designs are faulty and Bloggs complied with all Classit's requirements, Bloggs would have a defence under the Act.

When must a claim be brought?

There are two matters to note here:

(a) In respect of personal injuries or property damage, the injured individual generally has three years in which to institute claim. Schedule 1, para. 1 amending 1980 Limitation Act.

(b) As far as the manufacturer is concerned, there is a 10 year cut-off point from the time he supplied the product to the retailer. Manufacturers will therefore have to keep good records of all their transactions.

From a practical point of view, insurance is going to assume a much greater importance in this area, as are well drafted indemnity clauses between persons in the distribution chain.

Recall notices

Rarely a day goes by without seeing a recall notice for a product in a local or national newspaper. A recall notice cannot relieve a manufacturer of liability under the Act, he has still produced a defective product. However there can be a reduction in damages on the grounds of contributory negligence if the consumer carried on using the product when he was aware of the recall.

6. EXCLUSION NOTICES

As has been seen, the Sale of Goods Act, the Supply of Goods (Implied Terms) Act, and the Supply of Goods and Services Act, give the buyer many rights in terms of description, merchantability, fitness for purpose and the kind of service that can be expected.

What is the effect if the seller or the supplier attempts to escape his obligations, *i.e.* to exclude liability? What if the shopper is confronted with notices such as:

> "Once the goods have left the store we accept no responsibility for them"
> "No refunds"
> "No returns"
> "Unless you return goods within 48 hours we will not entertain any complaints about the goods we sell"

When taking a film to be developed, consumers are often met with a standard clause such as:

> "in the event of loss, our liability is limited to the cost of a replacement film"

When walking in a store car park, the customer often sees notices such as:

> "We accept no responsibility for damage or injuries caused to consumers using this car park howsoever caused"

It can be seen that the effect of all of these clauses is that someone is trying to escape liability.

Can this be done?

Firstly, the starting point for all exclusion clauses is to see whether or not they have been *incorporated into* the contract, for if incorporation has not occurred the clauses have no effect.

The common law rules as to incorporation must be considered.

1. If a consumer signs a document they are bound by it, in the absence of

   (a) misrepresentation – *Curtis* v. *Chemical Cleaning Co.* 1951 1 K.B. 805;
   (b) the *non est factum* rule.

The basic rule therefore is that once consumers have signed they are bound by the terms.

   (a) If the term is contained in an unsigned document, *e.g.* contained on a ticket or notice, the terms will only form part of the contract if reasonable steps were taken to bring it to the notice of the other party before the contract is made.
   (b) In an unsigned document, if the term is particularly onerous or unusual, it must be drawn to the other party's attention otherwise the term will not be incorporated, *Interfoto Picture*

Library v. *Stiletto* 1988. Here, the defendants found themselves with a bill for almost £4,000 when they retained some transparencies beyond a stated date. Unknown to them, the cost of keeping them beyond the date was £5.00 plus VAT per slide per day and as nearly 50 slides were involved, the bill totalled almost £4,000. The Court of Appeal held this onerous term had never been incorporated and the defendants could pay on a quantum meruit basis.

2. The type of document involved, *e.g.* the famous deck chair case of *Chapelton* v. *Barry UDC* 1940 will be considered. Here, a receipt could not be expected to contain vitally important exclusion clauses. There was no incorporation.

3. Sometimes exclusion clauses which, for a first time consumer might not be incorporated into a contract, could be incorporated by a course of dealings. See dicta in *Spurling* v. *Bradshaw* 1956; *McCutcheon* v. *David MacBrayne* 1964. Students should therefore watch out for questions such as: "Joe has purchased furniture from Sell it Fast on a number of occasions. Each time, after he has paid, he was given a piece of paper with much small print. He never bothered reading it and always threw it away as he left the store." There is a possibility in answering a question like this, subject to what has been said above, that the clause could have been incorporated by a course of dealings.

4. Does the clause cover the event which has occurred? Students should remember their contract law and doctrines, such as the contra preferentum rule. However, since the advent of the 1977 Unfair Contract Terms Act, the courts seem to have placed less importance on these older doctrines and more on the construction of the Act.

5. Unless students are given a choice, "a two tier" question, where they can answer one part as if incorporation has occurred and one part where it has not occurred, then the question should always be answered on the basis that incorporation has occurred. Marks are bound to have been allocated for a discussion of the Unfair Contract Terms Act, and students who opt for non-incorporation will only lose out.

THE UNFAIR CONTRACT TERMS ACT 1977

Points to note

1. The Unfair Contract Terms Act, where it operates:

(a) has the effect of making certain exclusion clauses void;

(b) has the effect of making certain clauses subject to the reasonableness test.

2. The Act governs any clause which purports to restrict or avoid liability. Section 13 Unfair Contract Terms Act (U.C.T.A.).

3. The Act does not *create* new duties, it merely controls clauses which cut down a duty.

4. The major provisions of the Act (ss.2–7) with the exception of section 6, only apply to business liability (U.C.T.A., s.1(3)). The Act is primarily designed to "get at" businesses who are trying to exclude liability, not at private individuals.

5. Schedule 1 of the Act contains a number of cases where the Act will not apply. The most important are contracts of insurance and any contract relating to the creation, transfer or termination of an interest in land.

Where does the Act operate?

So far as examinations are concerned, and in practice, the Act operates in *three major areas*:

1. Where exclusions in relation to the implied terms sections 13 and 14 of Sale of Goods Act 1979 (and their equivalents in the 1973 Supply of Goods (Implied Terms) Act and the 1982 Supply of Goods and Services Act) are concerned, *e.g.* "once the goods have left the store, we take no responsibility for them." "No refunds under any circumstances."

2. The person supplying the goods or services is trying to exclude their negligence based liability. Remember that section 13 of the Supply of Goods and Services Act says a service has to be supplied with reasonable care and skill. If a trader tries to exclude liability for the way in which the work has been performed, he is trying to exclude his negligence based liability, *e.g.* a garage has a notice which states:

"once the cars have left our premises any accidents are the responsibility of the customer. We accept no liability."

3. The person supplying the goods or services is trying to exclude liability for any other breach of contract, *e.g.* a clause in a removal contract limiting liability for breakages to £40 per item or for delay to £100. (The terms in removal contracts are currently under investigation by the Office of Fair Trading.)

The implied terms

Any attempt to exclude liability for a breach of the implied terms in sections 13 and 14 is void *where the buyer is dealing as a consumer*, (U.C.T.A., s.6).

What is dealing as a consumer?

Section 12 of the Unfair Contract Terms Act defines dealing as a consumer as:

"a party deals as a consumer if:

(a) he neither makes the contract in the course of a business nor holds himself out as doing so; and

(b) the other party does make the contract in the course of a business; and

(c) the goods passing under the contract are of a type ordinarily supplied for private use or consumption."

Therefore, if Joanna, a private individual, purchases a washing machine from Bewis's, a discount store, Joanna is dealing as a consumer. If, when she purchased the machine, she signed an invoice which stated no refunds given under any circumstances, this is clearly an attempt to exclude liability for merchantability, *i.e.* section 14 of the Sale of Goods Act. Joanna satisfies the definition of dealing as a consumer, therefore the clause is void and Joanna can sue for a breach of merchantable quality.

Points to note

(a) The onus is on the retailer to show that the other party to the contract is dealing as a non-consumer (s.12(3)). So, in the example given above, the burden of proof is on Bewis's to show that Joanna is a non-consumer.

(b) Dealing as a consumer has been discussed most recently in the Court of Appeal decision in *R. & B. Customs Brokers Ltd.* v. *U.D.T.* 1988.

In this case a car was purchased in the name of the Plaintiff Ltd. Company whose purpose in trading was freight loading. The car was purchased for the managing director's use. It was not essential to the running of the business, nor could any regular practice of buying cars for directors be established. It will be recalled that the car had a leaky roof and, although it was of merchantable quality, there was a breach of section 14(3) *i.e.* that the car was not reasonably fit for its purpose. The contract between the plaintiffs and the defendants contained exclusion clauses. If it could be found that the plaintiff buyer was dealing as a consumer, these clauses would be void. Remember the car was bought in the limited company's name. The Court of Appeal held that where the activity was not an *integral* part of the business (as here) and where no degree of regularity could be found (as here) then the plaintiffs could not be said to be acting in the course of a business. The plaintiffs therefore satisfied all the requirements of section 12. They were therefore dealing as consumers and the clause seeking to exclude liability for section 14(3) was declared void. Students should not therefore assume that every time a limited company purchases goods that they are always acting "in the course of a business."

(c) If it is a hire purchase transaction then once again if the buyer deals as a consumer the equivalents of sections 13 and 14 in the Supply of Goods (Implied Terms) Act, 1973 *i.e.* sections 9 and 10 can never be excluded. Again, this is by virtue of section 6 of U.C.T.A.

Where the buyer deals as a non-consumer, a clause excluding the implied terms under sections 13 and 14 of the Sale of Goods Act is subject to the reasonableness test.

The reasonableness test

Schedule 2 of U.C.T.A. lays down a *non-exhaustive* list of guidelines, these include:

(a) the strength of the bargaining position between the parties;
(b) whether any inducement to agree to the term;
(c) whether the customer knew of the term;
(d) whether the goods were specially manufactured.

Again, the onus of proving the clause is reasonable lies on the party seeking to rely upon it.

The following cases serve to illustrate how the reasonableness test has been looked at by the courts.

Mitchell v. *Finney Lock Seeds* 1983 2 A.C. 803

Here the buyers purchased 30 lb of Dutch cabbage seed for £201.60. There was an exemption clause limiting the sellers' liability to the cost of replacement seeds in the event of loss. The seeds turned out to be of the incorrect variety and the buyers lost thousands of pounds in profits. Indeed by the time the claim reached the House of Lords the claim stood at approximately £100,000!

Remember, the guidelines in Schedule 2 are non-exhaustive. Looking purely from the point of view was the clause reasonable, the courts decided not on the basis that:

(a) it was the sellers' fault;

(b) they had in previous cases paid out more than replacement value;
(c) they could have insured against loss.

The buyers therefore won their claim.

Many cases involving reasonableness have arisen out of the developing of photographs. In *Woodman* v. *Photo Trade Processing* (1981) *New L.J.* 935, the Defendants accepted films for developing and printing on the basis that the value of such material did not exceed the cost of the material itself and that the developer's liability was limited to the cost of a replacement film. The photographs in question were wedding photos. The Plaintiff received back only 13 negatives. The remaining 23 had been lost. The court decided that the clause seeking to limit liability was unreasonable and awarded £75 damages for distress and disappointment. There does not appear to have been a problem on incorporation but the court clearly thought that most consumers would not take much notice of the clause and that the retailers should not be allowed to rely on it. However, the question was posed, what if the developer provided an alternative, *i.e.* offered merely a replacement film for normal developing rates, but if the consumer paid more he would obtain a higher level of cover. This is sometimes known as the "two tier" option.

This question was answered in two cases, both reported in *Which*.

(a) *Warren* v. *TRUPRINT* (September 1986);
(b) *McQuade* v. *TESCO* (November 1988).

In both cases consumers took photographs of important family occasions. When they took them to the developers there was the usual standard clause as outlined above, plus a clause that if a supplementary charge was paid, a higher level of protection would be given. In neither case was the extra charge paid, in both cases the film was lost and in both cases the argument was, did the second clause demanding the extra charge have the effect of making the replacement film clause reasonable.

In both cases the courts felt that consumers would not, just before handing films over (or sending them through the post) hold back and ask for details of an extra service fee. If the fee was prominently set out or details pointed out then the situation could be different.

In a recent survey done by the Watchdog BBC Consumer programme in 1992 to discover exactly what the extra charges were, researchers received either no response from the major developing firms or a complete surprise reaction that the question had ever been asked. This clearly supports the court's view that consumers do not ask the question either!

In both cases the courts decided the clause was unreasonable and in both cases the plaintiffs received £50 damages for distress and disappointment.

In *Gore* v. *Thomson* (reported in the Weekend Telegraph 1992) the courts decided that when Mr. Gore's holiday plans were changed at short notice, the exclusion clause relied on by the operator was judged to be unreasonable.

Some other cases involving reasonableness which are worth considering are:

(a) *Smith* v. *Eric Bush* 1990;
(b) *Walker* v. *Boyle* 1982;
(c) *Phillips Products Ltd.* v. *Hyland* 1987.

The case of *Stewart Gill Ltd.* v. *Horatio Myer & Co. Ltd.* 1992 is also worthy of note. It is a commercial rather than a consumer case, but the decision may be relevant to consumer cases in the future. Here the plaintiffs who were trying to enforce payment had a clause in the contract which stated "the Customer shall not be entitled to withhold payment of any amount due to the company under the contract by reason of any payment credit set off counterclaim allegation of incorrect or defective goods *or for any other reason whatsoever*" – On an interlocutory claim the court decided these last few words rendered the whole clause unreasonable, the inference being that if the clause would have been drafted differently, and not so widely, then parts of it may have been allowed to stand in another form. Clearly the longer and more complicated the clause, the more chance the *whole* lot stands to be struck out whereas if it is split into Clauses 1, 2 and 3 for example, some clauses may survive the reasonableness test.

Terms in the supply of goods and services act

So far the Sale of Goods implied terms have been discussed and their equivalents under the Supply of Goods (Implied Terms) Act. What of the implied terms relating to goods governed by the Supply of Goods and Services Act, *i.e.* exchange goods, hire goods or the materials part of a works and materials contract.

Section 7 of the Unfair Contract Terms Act says in relation to these implied terms then, as in section 6, any attempt to exclude them is void where the buyer deals as a consumer and, subject to the reasonableness test, where the buyer is a non-consumer.

In other words *section 7* works in exactly the same way as *section 6*. All a student has to know is that if the Supply of Goods and Services Act is involved then, in relation to the goods part, it is U.C.T.A., s.7 which must be used and not section 6. Thus, if Fred takes his car into a garage to have it serviced, and defective parts have been used and there is an exclusion clause on the signed invoice excluding liability for work and materials, then in respect of the materials, liability cannot be excluded by section 7 where Fred is dealing as a consumer. This work and materials example will be considered at the end of the next section on negligence.

Negligence based clauses

The second important area where U.C.T.A. operates is in relation to negligence based clauses.

Negligence is defined in section 1 as the breach of a duty of care arising in contract. This includes the section 13 of the Supply of Goods and Services Act term. It also includes the breach of a duty of care in tort or breach of the common duty of care under the Occupiers Liability Act 1957.

As far as Consumer Law is concerned, the area which is most likely to arise in examinations is an attempt to exclude liability for a breach of section 13 of the Supply of Goods and Services Act. This is a clear attempt to exclude liability for negligence. Section 2 of the Unfair Contract Terms Act says that any clause or notice is ineffective, *i.e.* void insofar as it attempts to exclude liability for negligence resulting *in death or personal injury*. Thus, in the example given earlier, where Fred has his car serviced, suppose this time the parts were not defective but the installation was incorrect. Fred again has a signed invoice excluding liability for work and materials. On his way home, due to the poor workmanship, the brakes failed and he crashed causing himself personal injury. He can sue for a breach of section 13 of Supply of Goods and Services Act. Once negligence has been proven (Do remember this requirement, for if Fred could not prove defective workmanship, there would be no breach of an implied term) then any exclusion clause would be void as the end result damage is personal injury.

Section 2(2) of the Unfair Contract Terms Act goes on to state that if any other loss or damage results then the clause of notice is only valid provided the reasonableness test as outlined earlier is satisfied.

Therefore, if Fred is dissatisfied with the way in which the work has been performed, but does not have a crash and takes the car to be repaired elsewhere, costing him say £100, he could attempt to recover his £100 and any exclusion clause brought in by the first garage would be subject to the reasonableness test as Fred has only suffered financial loss.

It is most important when answering questions involving work and materials to split the answer up as to whether the damage is caused by the work or the materials or both. Remember, if it is the materials and an exclusion, section 7 of the Unfair Contract Terms Act operates, if it is work and there is an exclusion section 2 of the Unfair Contract Terms Act operates.

Other breaches of contract

The third major area where U.C.T.A. operates is in relation to other breaches of contract, *i.e.* any other clause in a contract. This is governed by section 3 of U.C.T.A.

Section 3 applies where one party deals as a consumer or on the other party's written standard terms of business.

The section applies to a clause whereby that other party:

(a) tries to exclude or restrict his liability in respect of a breach of contract, *e.g.* liability limited to £100 or as in the photo cases liability limited to the cost of a replacement film.

or

(b) claims to be entitled to render a contractual performance substantially different from that which was reasonably expected of him, *e.g.* where the management reserve the right to alter any performance or a tour company to alter a holiday.

or

(c) claims to be entitled to render no performance at all, *e.g.* seller not liable for non-delivery.

All these clauses are subject to the reasonableness test. Thus it can now be seen why in the photograph cases outlined earlier, the clauses were subject to the reasonableness test.

These are the three most important areas to be dealt with by U.C.T.A.

Other provisions of the Unfair Contract Terms Act

The Act also contains other provisions relating to exclusion clauses.

(a) By section 4 a person dealing as a consumer cannot be made to indemnify another person against liability for negligence or breach of contract unless the clause satisfies the reason-ableness test.

(b) Section 5 deals with manufacturers' guarantees and declares that if goods which are ordinarily supplied for private use or consumption prove defective while in consumer use and cause loss or damage as a result of negligence in manufacture or distribution, then any attempt to exclude liability in a guarantee is void.

(c) If a misrepresentation is involved, then any attempt to exclude liability for misrepresentation is only valid provided the reasonableness test is satisfied. Section 3 of 1967 Misrepresentation Act as amended by section 8 of U.C.T.A.

Criminal liability for exemption clauses

Up to this point only civil liability has been considered in relation to exclusion clauses. The clauses however may involve the seller in criminal liability and it is always worth considering whether extra marks could be gained by bringing these factors into question.

The Consumer Transactions (Restrictions on Statements) Order 1976 as amended, makes it a criminal offence to use a void exemption clause in a consumer sale of goods or hire purchase contract. Therefore a notice such as no refunds on any goods sold would render the seller criminally liable. Of course, under the civil law if the consumer purchased defective goods, then by using section 6 of U.C.T.A. the clause would be void. Note, the order does not apply to transactions governed by the 1982 Supply of Goods and Services Act so although clauses here can be dealt with under the civil law they would not be illegal. Also clauses excluding liability for damage resulting from negligence may be void or unreasonable, but they are not illegal.

In *Hughes* v. *Hall* (1981) R.T.R. 430 a notice "sold as seen and inspected" was declared illegal, but in *Cavendish & Woodhouse* v. *Manley* (1984) 148 J.P. 289 "sold as seen" was held not to contravene the order.

The order also makes it an offence to supply goods to a consumer with written exclusion clauses without pointing out that a consumer's statutory rights are unaffected; or even if an exclusion clause is not mentioned, if extra rights are given, the person giving those rights must make it clear that other statutory rights are unaffected. This is why manufacturers, when they offer to replace goods free of charge, *e.g.* soup, confectionery, must place a statement nearby saying statutory rights are unaffected as of course the consumer's rights in contract are against the store and not against the manufacturer.

The EEC intervention

In relation to Unfair Contract Terms like many other areas of Consumer Protection there are attempts to standardise liability throughout the Community.

There is a European Directive on Unfair Terms in *Consumer* contracts which, according to a Press Release P/93/111 issued by the Department of Trade and Industry "will introduce for the first time a general concept of fairness into UK and European Law which the consumer has not had the opportunity to negotiate."

Baroness Denton said in the release that The Unfair Contract Terms Directive will help correct the disadvantages many individuals are under in dealing with large corporations which offer their goods and services on a "take it or leave it" basis.

It is an important step forward as it will mean that standard form contracts which have written into them a significant imbalance in the parties' rights to the detriment of the consumer will be outlawed.

Points to note

(a) The draft directive is concerned only with contracts between business suppliers and consumers;
(b) the 1977 Act protects businesses;
(c) no contracts are excluded from the draft Directive;
(d) it concentrates on the word fairness rather than reasonableness;
(e) it does appear that the whole contract and not just the term complained of will be considered when deciding if the term is fair although again there is much argument on this. Article 4(1);
(f) where a term is judged to be unfair, it is void.

The Directive passed through the Council on April 5, 1993, but has yet to be enacted and become formally part of English law. A consultation period is to be given to discuss the Directive with interested parties. The Directive is meant to be enacted before December 31, 1994.

Summary

The Unfair Contract Terms Act is complicated. A summary of its most important provisions is outlined below:

Clauses made void

(a) Where the buyer deals as a consumer the implied terms under sections 13 and 14 of Sale of Goods Act, sections 9 and 10 of the Supply of Goods (Implied Terms) Act 1973, sections 3 and 4 of the Supply of Goods and Services Act (U.C.T.A., ss.6 and 7).

(b) Manufacturers' guarantees (U.C.T.A., s.5).

(c) An attempt to exclude liability for death or personal injury resulting from negligence (U.C.T.A., s.2).

Clauses made subject to the reasonableness test

(a) Where the buyer deals as a non-consumer the implied terms under sections 13 and 14 of Sale of Goods Act, sections 9 and 10 of the Supply of Goods (Implied Terms) Act 1973, sections 3 and 4 of the Supply of Goods and Services Act (U.C.T.A., ss.6 and 7);

(b) Indemnity clauses;

(c) An attempt to exclude liability for misrepresentation;

(d) Contractual clauses governed by U.C.T.A., s.3;

(e) An attempt to exclude liability for negligence where property damage or financial damage results.

---

7. CONSUMER CREDIT

The issues mentioned so far have not involved any discussion of how most consumers finance their purchases and if they do use some form of credit, then how does this affect the transaction and are they given a higher level of protection.

The Consumer Credit Act 1974 was enacted in an attempt to regulate the whole credit industry. It is not the purpose of this text to give a historical analysis of the problems facing the credit industry and consumers, rather this introductory chapter into Credit will attempt to set out clearly and concisely the aid given to consumers by the legislation. It is *impossible* to understand the Consumer Credit Act 1974 and its effect on consumers without an appreciation of how basic credit transactions operate and what the definitions in the 1974 Act actually mean.

First, the aims of the 1974 Act are:

(a) To regulate the formation, terms and enforcement of credit and hire agreements. It gives consumers many rights and places certain restraints upon the enforcement of an agreement against a consumer.

(b) It sets up a licensing system whereby those engaged in any form of consumer credit business must be licensed. The licensing system applies to many ancillary businesses.

(c) It has provisions designed to secure truth in lending, showing the true cost of credit and the true annual rate of interest.

(d) It controls door to door canvassing for credit and creates a number of criminal offences in order to prevent other undesirable methods of seeking credit business.

(e) The Director-General of Fair Trading, Sir Bryan Carsberg, has the task of administering the licensing system and the general enforcement of the Act. Other enforcement powers are given to Local Trading Standards Officers.

(f) It is impossible to contract out the provisions of the Act as a result of section 173 of The Consumer Credit Act.

Let us therefore look at regulation first of all. As stated earlier, it is impossible to understand credit without a basic appreciation of how various credit transactions work. Once this is understood, then the definitions will be applied. With this in mind, a number of examples have been selected to work through. The examples chosen are:

(a) A hire purchase agreement;
(b) A conditional sale agreement;
(c) A credit sale agreement;
(d) Buying goods or services using a credit card;
(e) Using a credit card to obtain cash to buy goods or services;
(f) Obtaining a loan to buy goods or services and arriving at the lender via the person who supplied the goods or services;
(g) Obtaining a personal loan from a bank or other financial institution;
(h) Using an overdraft facility.

These are the most common types of credit transactions to occur in Consumer Law examinations.

1. Hire purchase

This is a bailment of goods with an option to purchase. What happens in practice is that the consumer (the debtor) wishes to purchase a car, for example from Black and White's Garage, but cannot afford to buy outright. Black and White do all their financing on hire purchase terms via Grasping Finance Ltd. The debtor normally conducts all his negotiations via the garage, selects his car and fills in an offer form with all his financial details. The form is then passed on to the finance company who will check on the debtor's creditworthiness and provided they are satisfied will "accept" the deal. The garage then sells the car to the finance company and it is the finance company who bail the goods out to the debtor with an option to purchase. The debtor therefore is actually contracting with the finance company *not* the garage for the purchase of the vehicle, so that if the car proves to be defective the debtor's rights under the Supply of Goods (Implied Terms) Act 1973 are exercisable against the finance company. Diagram 1 serves to illustrate this and is known as the *Hire Purchase Triangle*.

Diagram 1: A Hire Purchase Agreement

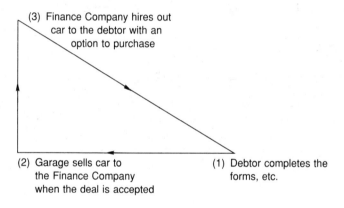

(3) Finance Company hires out car to the debtor with an option to purchase

(2) Garage sells car to the Finance Company when the deal is accepted

(1) Debtor completes the forms, etc.

Note: the debtor is in contract with the Finance Company.

2. Conditional sale agreement

This is a sale of goods subject to a condition and the condition is that the property will not pass until the goods have been paid for. As in Hire Purchase the finance company has legal title to the goods until the last instalment is paid.

A conditional sale agreement works in exactly the same way as a hire purchase agreement, exactly the same steps take place in the transaction and the debtor is once again contracting with the finance company. The only difference to note is that the transaction is governed by the Sale of Goods Act 1979 and *not* the Supply of Goods (Implied Terms) Act 1973.

Diagram 2: A Conditional Sale Agreement

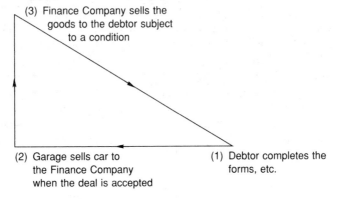

(3) Finance Company sells the
goods to the debtor subject
to a condition

(2) Garage sells car to
the Finance Company
when the deal is accepted

(1) Debtor completes the
forms, etc.

Note: the debtor is in contract with the Finance Company.

3. Credit sale agreement

This situation usually occurs when a store is financing its own goods to increase sales. If it is a credit sale agreement then the property passes to the debtor immediately so that, unlike a conditional sale or hire purchase agreement, the finance company has no rights over the goods. Rather than a triangle, as the store is doing its own financing, the credit sale diagram can be done in a straight line:

[1] Debtor agrees to buy goods ——▶— [2] Store supplies goods and the credit

Store = Financier **and** Supplier

The transaction, if it is for goods, is governed by the Sale of Goods Act. It could well be that the consumer could be buying services, *e.g.* building work, which he is going to pay for over a number of months. This time, the builder is financing the deal and the transaction is governed by the Supply of Goods and Services Act 1982.

4. Buying goods or services using a credit card

When using a credit card to buy goods or services, the consumer is entering into a contract with the store or the supplier of the work to supply the goods or services. He agrees to pay his credit card off and the store/supplier sends his credit voucher to the company who will pay out the value less any agreed commission rates.

Diagram 3

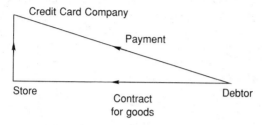

Credit Card Company

Payment

Store

Contract
for goods

Debtor

The steps taken are:

(a) Contract between the store and the debtor governed by the Sale of Goods Act 1979 (or, if for services by the Supply of Goods and Services Act 1982);

(b) Store sends off voucher to credit card company for reimbursement less commission charges. (May be done via other electronic means but important point is that the retailer is reimbursed.)

(c) Debtor owes the credit card company the amount for goods or services.

5. Using a credit card to obtain cash

When the credit card is used to withdraw cash, the debtor agrees according to his contract with the credit card company to repay the cash, plus usually a handling charge for the facility (VISA and ACCESS currently charge 1.5 per cent. This charge arises from the date of cash withdrawal, and not from the statement date).

When the money is used to purchase goods or services, separate contracts come into existence with the various suppliers:

(a) Debtor uses card to withdraw cash. He owes the money to the credit card company.

(b) Debtor enters into entirely separate contracts for the purchase of goods or services.

6. Obtaining a loan where the loan company is linked to the supplier of the goods or services

When this situation occurs the debtor agrees to purchase goods or services from, *e.g.* a garage. The garage has an arrangement with the finance company whereby the finance company agrees to loan all the garage's clients money to purchase cars. This is known as a *loan linked agreement.* The company loans the debtor the money (1 contract) and the debtor purchases the goods from the garage (2nd contract). The loan company usually settles the amount outstanding direct with the garage. The sale contract between the debtor and the garage is governed by the Sale of Goods Act 1979.

Diagram 4

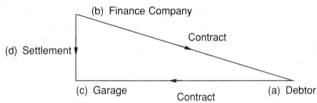

(a) Debtor agrees to buy goods;
(b) Contract between loan company and debtor;
(c) Sale contract between debtor and garage;
(d) Settlement between garage and finance company.

7. Obtaining a personal loan

Here there is no link between the garage and the finance company. The debtor agrees to purchase the car and the first contract is governed by the Sale of Goods Act 1979. Let us say for instance that he obtained a loan from The Good Bank Ltd. to finance the transaction. This second contract is a loan and the money is generally credited to the debtor's account.

Diagram 5

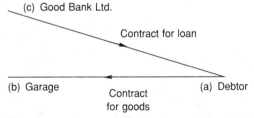

(a) Debtor agrees to purchase goods;
(b) The deal between the debtor and the garage is a contract governed by the Sale of Goods Act;
(c) Loan agreement by bank and debtor is a second contract.

8. Overdraft facilities

Here, the debtor has entered into a contract whereby a bank will loan him money up to an agreed limit subject to repayment terms. However the debtor chooses to spend his money, there is no connection between the bank and the suppliers of the goods or services.

---

8. CONSUMER CREDIT: DEFINITIONS

The eight examples outlined in the previous chapter are the most common types of credit transactions which will be encountered in examinations and practice.

The next stage of understanding and appreciating how credit works is to master the definitions under the Consumer Credit Act.

Definitions

The definitions are contained in sections 8–20 of the Act and they are vital to answering Consumer Credit questions. Most of the controls under the Act apply only to a *"regulated"* agreement. To discover whether an agreement is *regulated* it must come within the definition of a consumer credit agreement contained in section 8 of the Act. The agreement, provided it satisfies section 8 is a regulated one as long as it is not exempt under section 16. In other words, the Act does not say what a regulated (a covered agreement under the Act) agreement is, it merely states which agreements are not covered under the Act. If an agreement satisfies section 8 and is not exempt, it is regulated. It is impossible to understand what constitutes an exempt agreement until the definitions are understood, therefore via a circular route we are able to reach the definition of a regulated agreement.

Firstly, the definition under section 8 will be considered, then the remaining definitions will be looked at in the context of the eight examples given in the previous chapter so that the student will become used to categorising agreements immediately and understand the importance of the definitions.

Monetary limits

The starting point for all agreements is to consider the effect of section 8 for section 8 of the Consumer Credit Act defines an agreement. It says it is an agreement by which the creditor provides the individual (and the word individual includes a partnership *but not* a company) with credit not exceeding £15,000. (The original limit of £5,000 set out in the Act now stands by virtue of regulations at £15,000.) The monetary limit is therefore the first significant factor to be considered when deciding whether or not an agreement is covered by the Act.

The Act covers agreements where the amount of credit extended is less than £15,000. Many creditors nowadays choose to lend more than £15,000 so that they are not concerned with the Consumer Credit Act and often advertisements will appear stating that the lender will only lend in excess of £15,001.

Fixed sum and running account credit

Often agreements will have a total repayment well in excess of £15,000 when deposits and interest charges are taken into account *but* the significant figure for determining whether or not it is covered by the Act brings in the first definition to be considered, *i.e.* fixed sum credit. Therefore:

(a) If it is fixed sum credit the *significant* figure for determining whether the agreement is within the monetary limits is to consider the amount of money being lent *not* the end result figure on the agreement. *Fixed Sum Credit* is where the amount being lent can be determined at the outset by both the debtor and the creditor so that in the examples given earlier: hire purchase; conditional sales; credit sales; loan linked and independent loan agreements, these are all examples of fixed sum credit as the debtor signs an agreement to repay a fixed amount of money. Therefore the significant figure is the amount of money being lent so that if Jack agrees to buy a car on hire purchase terms for a total price of £20,000 and the figure includes interest charges of £4,000 and a deposit of £3,000 the actual amount of money being lent is £13,000. The agreement is therefore within the Act. Do *not* therefore be misled into starting a question with the words "as the total price exceeds £15,000 the agreement is not covered," remember the *significant* figure is the amount being lent.

(b) Credit is either fixed sum or running account. Fixed sum has just been covered. If the credit is running account, this means that the debtor is given a pre-set credit limit by the creditor and is allowed to "run up" to that amount. Thus, in the examples given earlier, credit cards used to pay for goods and services, or to withdraw cash and overdraft facilities, are all examples of running account credit. Here the significant figure for determining whether it is within the Act is the credit limit. If it is below £15,000 the agreement is covered by the Act. Therefore most credit cards are covered under this provision.

Running account and fixed sum credit are defined under the Act in section 10. Because it was felt that some creditors might set artificially high credit limits to avoid the Act, section 10(3) sets out that running account credit will still qualify as a regulated consumer credit agreement if:

(a) The debtor cannot withdraw more than £15,000 at any one time;

(b) the debtor exceeds a certain amount and the rate of interest becomes very high;

(c) at the time of making the agreement it is unlikely that the debit balance will ever exceed £15,000.

Thus, it can be seen that even if the credit limit is higher, the agreement may still be covered by the Act. Credit cards should always be studied to see whether or not they are covered by the full protection of the Act. A number of *gold* cards issued by the leading banks may not be covered under the Act because of the amount limits set out in this section.

Restricted use and unrestricted use credit

The next definition to be considered is that the agreement must either be restricted use credit or unrestricted use credit (C.C.A., s.11). If the debtor's use to which he can put the credit is in some way restricted by the creditor, then the credit is restricted use. As a rough guide if the debtor is able to place his hands on the money it is unrestricted use credit.

To take some examples in a hire purchase, conditional sale or credit sale: the creditor will only lend the debtor the money provided that certain goods or services are purchased using it. The debtor ends up with the goods, but never has any money in his hand therefore credit sales, conditional sales and hire purchase are all restricted use credit. When a credit card is used to buy goods or services the debtor's use to which he can put the card is restricted to those outlets which will take the card. He is therefore obtaining restricted use credit (albeit he can use the card in thousands of outlets) and again never has any money in his hand.

In the case of a loan linked agreement (Example 6, above), the loan company will usually settle direct with the garage. Thus, again it is restricted use credit and the debtor does not receive the money. Where a credit card is used to withdraw cash to pay for goods or services, the credit is unrestricted, the debtor has money in his hand and is free to spend it wherever he chooses.

In the case of a personal loan agreement, the bank credits the debtor with the agreed amount and the debtor writes out a cheque to the garage for instance, in Example 7. The credit here is unrestricted use, as once the debtor has the money in his account, he is basically free to do with it whatever he wishes. This is so even if he is in breach of contract with the bank, section 11(3) because he has obtained the loan, for instance, for a car and has spent it on a holiday. (Of course the bank would only ever express an interest where the debtor failed to make his repayments.)

If, in the case of Example 6, the loan company did credit the account of the debtor and the debtor was to settle matters with the garage, again the credit would be unrestricted use, although the debtor acted properly. Overdraft facilities are of course always unrestricted use.

Debtor-creditor or debtor-creditor-supplier agreement

The next definition (and perhaps the most important one to be considered) is whether the agreement is a debtor-creditor-supplier agreement (referred to as a DCS agreement) or a debtor-creditor agreement (sometimes referred to as a DC agreement). Generally, the debtor achieves a much higher level of protection if his credit agreement can be classed as a debtor-creditor-supplier agreement.

It is *absolutely vital* to understand the Consumer Credit Act terminology. The word *supplier* means the person the debtor has *legally* contracted to obtain the goods or services from, *not* the person who actually hands them over. Therefore, in our hire purchase, conditional sale and credit sale examples, the legal supplier is the finance company and *not* the middle man garage or store. This point cannot be overemphasised.

For an agreement to be a debtor-creditor-supplier one under section 12 there has to be some kind of *business connection* between the supplier and the creditor. This arises in three ways under the Act and is again best illustrated by examples:

(i) Where the supplier and creditor are the same person (C.C.A., s.12(a))

In a hire purchase, conditional sale or credit sale agreement (Examples 1 to 3) the legal supplier of the goods, as stated above, is the finance company.

They are also the creditor. What stronger business connection could there be than that the creditor and supplier is the same person. Conditional sale, credit sale and hire purchase are always debtor-creditor-supplier agreements and, as the creditor and the supplier are the same, they are known as two party debtor-creditor-supplier agreements. Building up on the definitions learnt, hire purchase, credit sale and conditional sales are all examples of two party debtor-creditor-supplier agreements for restricted use fixed sum credit.

(ii) Where the supplier and the creditor operate under a restricted use credit agreement made under pre-existing arrangements These are loan linked agreements and credit cards used to purchase goods or services. In both cases the only way the debtor obtained credit to purchase the goods was because of some business arrangement in force between the supplier and the finance company. The only way a consumer can use his credit card in a store is because the store has an arrangement, *e.g.* with ACCESS or VISA. In these two cases (Examples 4 and 6) the creditor and the supplier are different persons so although the agreement in each case is a debtor-creditor-supplier one, this time it is a three party DCS agreement. Thus, loan linked agreements and credit cards can be fully categorised as three party debtor-creditor-supplier agreements for restricted use fixed sum (in the case of loans) or running account (in the case of credit cards) credit.

(iii)   Where unrestricted use credit is involved and where the creditor under pre-existing arrangements with the supplier credits the debtor, anticipating that the debtor will forward the cash onto the supplier This is an example of the loan linked agreement where the creditor credits the debtor and the debtor settles the account with the supplier. If this happens, again because the debtor only "came by" the money because of the link between the creditor and the supplier and used it as he ought to use it, he has created a debtor-creditor-supplier agreement. This one can be categorised as a three party DCS for unrestricted use fixed sum credit. It is comparatively rare compared to i) and ii) above as normally the finance Company settles direct with the supplier.

(iv)   All other agreements are debtor-creditor agreements as there is no link between the supplier and the creditor C.C.A., s.13. Thus where credit cards are used to withdraw

cash or personal loans, or overdraft facilities are involved, these are all examples of debtor-creditor agreements.

Thus all credit agreements need to be categorised into:

    (a) Price limits;
    (b) Fixed sum or running account credit;
    (c) Restricted use or unrestricted use credit;
    (d) Debtor-creditor or debtor-creditor-supplier agreements;
    (e) Two or three party debtor-creditor-supplier agreements.

Always categorise agreements to pick up the maximum amount of marks.

Exempt agreements

Now that definitions have been learnt and understood via the circular route, section 16 has been reached, *i.e.* the definition of an exempt agreement. The following are the most important categories of an exempt agreement:

    (a) The first four exemptions relate to land mortgages. As a general rule most first land mortgages are outside the ambit of the Act and this text. A number of second mortgages not used to finance the purchase of land will come within the ambit of the Act but again, as they do not usually form the basis of examination questions, they will not be discussed here.

    (b) Debtor-creditor-supplier agreements (but not hire purchase or conditional sale agreements) for fixed sum credit, where the number of payments to be made by the debtor does not exceed four (excluding any deposit) and must be repaid within twelve months of the making of the agreement. It is the intention of this exemption to avoid creditors in much form filling, etc.

    (c) Debtor-creditor-supplier agreements for running account credit where the debtor has to repay the balance in a single payment. This affects cards like American Express and Diners Club where debtors have to repay the whole outstanding balance and cannot like in the case of VISA or ACCESS repay part and incur interest on the balance. The fact that these are exempt agreements is of vital importance if, for instance, the goods purchased with the cards are defective, because section 75 of the Consumer Credit Act does not apply as the agreement is not regulated. Students should always check in any examination question what kind of card is involved and if it is unclear, the answer should include a statement saying "Assuming the card is of the ACCESS/VISA variety, then the agreement is a consumer credit agreement for restricted use running accounting credit and is regulated as it is not exempt."

(d) Debtor-creditor agreements where the cost of credit is very low, *i.e.* where the annual percentage rate for the total charge for credit does not exceed the higher of 13 per cent. or 1 per cent. above the highest of any base rates published by the English and Scottish clearing banks. This exemption is intended to help creditors who lend at very low rates of interest avoid paperwork. It could arise in an employment situation where an employer makes a cheap loan, but is unlikely to arise in a normal commercial situation, although students may discover that some of their loan agreements could fall within the exception! The wording APR or annual percentage rate is the way lenders calculate how much interest a debtor has to pay on the amount of money borrowed. This has to be done to a formula set out by the Office of Fair Trading so that consumers can make a fair comparison amongst traders offering finance.

Very competitive pricing is currently taking place in the car industry and most manufacturers are advertising new cars at very highly subsidised rates of interest and more often than not at 0% APR. These are not covered by the exemption as they are of course *debtor-creditor-supplier* agreements.

Thus, once the exempted agreements are learnt, every other agreement where credit of less than £15,000 is lent is a regulated agreement.

Linked transactions

The final definition to be considered is that of a linked transaction. *Linked transactions are only important in relation to the debtor withdrawing from an agreement or cancelling an agreement.*

Linked transactions are defined by section 19 and include transactions entered into in compliance with the principal agreement, *e.g.* the debtor has to take out life insurance or car insurance if he wants the loan or, if it is a *three party* debtor-creditor-supplier agreement, then the supply agreement is a linked transaction in relation to the main agreement. This is set out in the diagram below.

Diagram 6

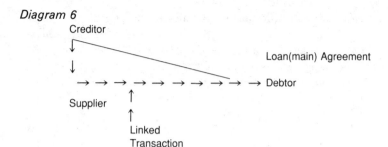

The purpose behind this is that if the debtor can escape from the main agreement then he wants to rid himself of any transactions linked to it.

In the following chapters, now that these definitions have been mastered, the most common kinds of questions both in examinations and practice will be considered.

---

9. CONSUMER CREDIT (3)

Once the basic definitions of consumer credit have been learnt, questions will arise in one of three ways. Students will be examined on issues of:

(a) How can a debtor escape as cheaply as possible from a credit agreement?
(b) The goods purchased on credit terms turn out to be defective.
(c) The debtor cannot afford to pay.

[there may be an overlap between (a) and (c)]

Licensing system

The Consumer Credit Act 1974 establishes a licensing system in an attempt to regulate the credit industry. This involves a system of issuing group licences for certain professions, (*e.g.* the Law Society) and standard individual licences. At the time of writing, the fees for a licence are £175 for a company and £70 for an individual or sole trader. The licences last for a period of five years.

The Director General can refuse an application for a licence or suspend a licence when he considers it fit to do so. According to the latest figures released by the Office of Fair Trading in 1993, 20,926 applications were received in 1992. Twenty thousand, five hundred and eighty-eight were issued, 172 notices were served on applicants or licence holders regarding their fitness to be granted or retain a licence. (Source: OFT Annual Report, 1993).

Licences are required by:

(a) anyone who lends money not in excess of £15,000 to individuals;

(b) anyone who passes an individual on to a source of finance (a credit broker.) This is the middle-man in many of the examples referred to earlier, *i.e.* the store or the garage;

(c) anyone who operates a credit-reference agency (these will be used to check on a person's creditworthiness);

(d) anyone who gives consumer debt advice.

Thus, the attempt to regulate the industry can be seen in that, not only are lenders caught by the Act, but also many ancillary activities.

Sanctions for not having a licence

The sanctions for operating without a licence are both civil and criminal but it is the civil aspect which will be concentrated upon here. If a lender operates without a licence when one is required, then if he wishes to enforce the agreement he will be unable to do so without a validating order from the Director General of Fair Trading Consumer Credit Act, s.40. In addition, if the credit broker is unlicensed but the creditor was licensed, once again the agreement is unenforceable without a validating order Consumer Credit Act, s.149. Consumer law students should therefore note how many stores and garages have signs indicating "licensed credit broker."

Therefore, whenever a debtor wishes to escape from an agreement, it is always worth checking on the register kept in London whether or not the creditor or credit broker has a valid licence. If they do not have one, the agreement is unenforceable. In 1992 the Director General made five validating orders. Up to August 1993, six validating orders have been made.

The formal requirements of credit agreements

It has been seen above that the aim of licensing is to control the credit industry as a whole. Our attention is now turned towards the control of individual agreements. The Consumer Credit Act, mainly in the form of regulations made under section 60 and section 65 of the Act, sets out the form credit agreements should take, the size and colour of the printing, etc and how many copies are required.

The objective of the legislation is to make sure that the debtor is fully aware of all his rights and obligations in as plain English as possible, and if further information is needed, whom he ought to contact etc.

Sanctions for failure to observe the regulations

If the creditor fails to comply with the formalities, the agreement is said to be "improperly executed." By section 65 of the Consumer Credit Act, the agreement cannot be enforced against the debtor without a court order.

Note the difference between licensing defects which require a validating order from the Director General, whereas formality defects require court orders. Sometimes the defect is regarded as being so bad that the courts have no power to make an order (see, *e.g.* cancellable agreements). This would be a case of the debtor having his cake and being able to eat it!

Formalities

Sections 60 and 61 enable regulations to be made to ensure the debtor is made aware of his obligations and rights. The many details are found in the Consumer Credit (Agreements) Regulations 1983. Agreements (depending on their type) should make it clear *inter alia*:

(a) the amount and timing of repayments;
(b) the Annual percentage Rate (APR) (total charge for credit);
(c) the protection and remedies available to the debtor under the Act.

The copy provisions

This must be learnt and again the student is reminded of the necessity of knowing contract law. The Act sets out when and how many copies of an agreement a debtor should receive. The provisions are contained in sections 62 and 63.

Let us take a typical hire purchase example to illustrate the effect of the formalities.

Martin wishes to purchase a new Trissan Car from Damalls under a hire purchase agreement. He will complete the forms at the garage with details of the car, his income and the anticipated monthly repayments. (See How a Hire Purchase Agreement Works, earlier.) At this stage Martin is merely making an offer to purchase the car. No formal contract is concluded until the information is passed onto the Finance Company and they have accepted him after checking out his creditworthiness. In Consumer Credit Act terminology, Martin's offer means that he has an "unexecuted" agreement of a prospective regulated agreement. Martin must, in this situation, be given a copy of what he has signed. (s.62(1).)

When the deal is accepted by the finance company, a copy of the executed agreement must be delivered or sent within seven days (s.63(2)).

Therefore if the agreement is *unexecuted at the outset* Martin should end up with *two* copies.

Suppose, however, it is sale time and instant credit is on offer. In a number of situations the garage/store will be authorised by either their own financier, or an outside creditor to conclude deals on the spot provided they do not exceed a certain amount and that certain basic credit checks are made then and there. In that case the agreement is executed, offer and acceptance has occurred, the debtor is bound and is entitled to just one copy of the agreement (s.63(1&2)).

Summary

Where the agreement is unexecuted the debtor receives *two* copies, where the agreement is executed only *one* copy is required to comply with the formalities.

In the case of a cancellable agreement (this is discussed below) changes are made to the copy provisions:

(a) every copy must contain a notice in the prescribed form, telling the debtor of the right of cancellation, how to exercise it, and to whom it should be sent;

(b) in cases where a second copy is required (*i.e.* where the agreement is unexecuted at the outset) the second copy must be sent by post (s.63(3), so that no pressure is put on the debtor);

(c) in cases where a second copy is not required (*i.e.* where the agreement is executed) then if the agreement is cancellable a notice detailing the cancellation rights must be sent through the post to the debtor within seven days.

In the case of a cancellable agreement, if the requirements of (a), (b) and (c) above are not complied with, the "unenforceability" sanction is particularly severe, *i.e.* the creditor will be unable to enforce the agreement (s.127(3)).

Withdrawal

One of the cheapest ways of escaping from an agreement is to argue that there is in fact no agreement in existence between the seller and buyer, *i.e.* that offer and acceptance have not occurred.

Looking back at the formalities; whenever a debtor enters into a credit agreement, remember, if the agreement is unexecuted at the time, the debtor is entitled to a copy of the offer he has made. Suppose Bill agreed yesterday to purchase a TV and video on hire purchase terms from Bewis's. Grasping Finance service all their agreements. The agreement is unexecuted. Today Bill consults you, saying he has made a mistake and wants to escape from the agreement. Provided his "offer" has not been accepted by the finance company he can withdraw from the agreement using basic contractual rules.

Obviously he has to notify the creditor (or the credit-broker, Bewis's) as notice of revocation must be given before acceptance. This notice can be given orally. This is the effect of section 57 of the Act. (*Note*: that as revocation must be communicated to the offeree before acceptance it would be bad advice to rely on the post alone as acceptance could occur before the letter is received.)

Cancellation

Assuming that the licensing requirements have been met and all the formalities properly complied with so that the agreement has been properly executed, the final "cheap" way of escaping from an agreement is to see whether or not it is a cancellable one.

Normally where offer and acceptance have occurred, the agreement is concluded and is binding on the parties. However, we are now about to discover a situation where, although all the elements of contract law appear to have been satisfied, the consumer debtor is able to escape from the agreement by virtue of the provisions of section 67 of the Consumer Credit Act.

Section 67 was originally drafted to "get at" doorstep sales and offer the pressurised consumer an escape route once he had been persuaded to sign an agreement. However, it has been drafted in wide terms and covers situations other than doorstep sales.

Firstly, what makes an agreement cancellable?

By section 67, where oral representations have taken place in antecedent negotiations in *the debtor's presence and* the agreement has been signed away from the trade premises of the creditor, the negotiator (*i.e.* the supplier or credit-broker) or a party to a linked transaction, then the agreement is cancellable.

Antecedent negotiations as defined by section 56 of the Consumer Credit Act includes anything said about the goods or credit by the creditor or the credit-broker or the supplier *in the debtor's presence.*

Telephone negotiations are therefore not covered as it is easy for the debtor to merely put the telephone down.

It is easy to fulfil the requirements of the first part of this section as, in most consumer transactions, the buyer will, for example, in buying a car, visit the car showroom and ask various things about the car. There have therefore been antecedent oral representations. Note the wording is antecedent representations and not misrepresentations.

The second requirement is that of signing away from the creditor's business premises, etc. Therefore, once the buyer is allowed to take the agreement home for signature, the agreement is cancellable even though no pressure has been placed on the buyer to sign. This is so even if the buyer is a sole trader and signs on his business premises.

Therefore, if Joanna wishes to purchase a television for £600 including interest charges from Electric Ltd. on a credit sale agreement, discusses the deal with the salesman and asks if she can take the forms home to check everything and then signs them at home, the agreement is cancellable. (From the trader's point of view, do not allow consumers to take forms away from the premises.) If Joe, a sole trader, wishes to buy a car but says he is too busy to sign the agreement and could a salesman "drop" it off at his office, the agreement would again be cancellable.

When does the cancellation or cooling off period start and how long does it last?

Remember, if the agreement was unexecuted then the debtor should receive, through the post, within seven days of acceptance, a second copy. Both the first and second copy should contain a notice of cancellation rights. If the agreement was executed at the outset, then although in normal circumstances no second copy is required, a separate notice of cancellation rights must be sent through the post to the debtor within seven days.

It is the receipt of either the second copy or notice which triggers the cooling off period. This period is five days following the day the second copy or notice was received, so that if Joe receives his notice on Saturday he has until Thursday evening to cancel.

Therefore, by the time Joe is able to cancel he may well, from a practical point of view, have had the goods for almost a fortnight.

The aim of cancellation is to restore the parties to the position they would have been in had the agreement never been concluded. Thus, goods are returned and payments handed back. It should be pointed out from the retailers point of view that:

(a) they should not allow the debtor to take the forms away and
    make agreements cancellable if it is at all possible not to do so;
(b) they certainly should not allow the debtor to take the goods
    away until the cooling off period has expired.

If they do, and the debtor cancels they will suffer as the goods can
no longer be classed as new.

Notice must be exercised in writing, section 69 (see difference
between this and notice of withdrawal). It is valid from the time of
posting (and even if it gets lost) and is normally served on the
creditor or the credit-broker or supplier or someone named in the
notice.

In the case of a debtor-creditor-supplier agreement, all monies paid
by the debtor must be returned to him. He must make the goods available for collection although he has no positive duty to redeliver. He
also has a 21 day duty of care in respect of the goods so any damage
caused through negligence must be paid for, section 72(8).

If the agreement is a three party debtor-creditor-supplier
agreement for restricted use credit, then the creditor and the supplier are jointly and severally liable to repay any monies, section
70(1)(c).

If there is a part exchange involved, particularly where cars are
concerned, then under section 73 once the debtor has cancelled the
agreement, the negotiator (the credit-broker or the supplier) must
hand back the part exchange car or its equivalent monetary value
within 10 days. Again if it is a three party debtor-creditor-supplier
agreement, both the creditor and the supplier are jointly and severally liable. In all cases outlined above, the debtor has a lien over
the goods until he receives all his money back.

Some examples will best illustrate these statutory provisions:

1. Vera chooses a car from Doug's Garage, to be financed by a
loan linked agreement with Ridley Finance Ltd. Doug takes Vera's
Bastra car in part exchange for £1,000 and the balance is financed
via the loan agreement: Vera takes delivery of her new car under a
cancellable agreement, has it for three days and then cancels. Vera
must make the car available for collection. Doug, or Ridley Finance
Ltd., must either return Vera's car or its monetary value within 10
days as this is a three party debtor-creditor-supplier agreement.
Any monies paid over by Ridley Finance Ltd. must be returned.

2. Gail buys a TV set from Ivystores, financed by a loan of £270
from Don Ltd., a connected lender. Gail pays a deposit of £30 and
takes delivery after paying her first instalment of £20 to Don Ltd.
She then cancels. This is a three party debtor-creditor-supplier

agreement. Gail must make the set available for collection. She is entitled to receive the £30 deposit back from either Don Ltd. or Ivystores as is the case with the £20 as they are both jointly and severally liable. If Gail would have damaged the set in any way she would have been liable for the cost of repair under section 72(8).

Any linked transactions are normally automatically cancelled but in two important instances, by virtue of Consumer Credit (Linked Transactions Exemptions Regulations 1983) the debtor will have to take positive steps to cancel. These are in respect of contracts of insurance and guarantee. So if any insurance was involved, the debtor will have to cancel it.

Cancellation of debtor creditor agreement

In the case of a mere debtor-creditor agreement, *i.e.* a loan that is cancellable, the debtor may cancel as before. All the transactions he has spent his loan monies on will stand as they are not linked transactions and he is liable to repay the monies (he cannot therefore have his cake and eat it!), but if he repays them within one month or by the first repayment date, then no interest charges will be incurred, section 71 of the C.C.A.

It can be seen that *section 71* is only of any value where the debtor has found another cheaper source of finance, or won the pools!

---

10. LIABILITY FOR DEFECTIVE GOODS PURCHASED ON CREDIT TERMS

The second most common situation that a debtor will complain about is that the goods he has purchased using credit turn out to be defective. Is there any way in which the creditor can become involved in an action for defective goods?

Let us approach the question by using a number of examples:

Using an overdraft

1. Martin purchases a television from Bumbelows for £300. He has an overdraft facility with the bank and withdraws the money to pay for the TV set.

The credit in this case is therefore supplied under a debtor-creditor agreement for unrestricted use running account credit.

There is no connection between the bank and Bumbelows. If the
television proves defective then Martin's only remedy lies under the
Sale of Goods Act 1979 against Bumbelows for a breach of the
condition of merchantable quality. There is no possible question of
involving the creditor.

Hire-purchase and conditional sale agreements

2. Martin purchases the television under a hire purchase agreement from Bumbelows. Grasping Finance Ltd. finance all their
transactions. The salesman told Martin that the set was the most
reliable model they had in stock. It broke down four times in the
first month and cannot be repaired. Martin has paid his first instalment of £40.

This time, due to the hire purchase triangle, Martin's contract is
with Grasping Finance Ltd. The hire purchase agreement is a two
party debtor-creditor-supplier agreement for restricted use fixed
sum credit.

Martin's rights are all exercisable against the finance company
for a breach of section 10 of Supply of Goods (Implied Terms) Act
1973 relating to merchantable quality and fitness.

Martin is entitled to reject the goods for a breach of section 10.
There is no doctrine or acceptance, only affirmation. He can recover
his £40 and is released from paying future instalments.

In addition it could be that the salesman at Bumbelows has made
various misrepresentations about the goods (it could however be
construed as mere salestalk). Using section 56 of the C.C.A., this
says that where a negotiator, (here the store) in antecedent negotiations (words spoken about the goods or credit before the conclusion
of the deal) makes representations about the goods then he does so
not only in his own capacity but as agent for the creditor. Liability
cannot be avoided for this provision so that the creditor is directly
liable for everything the salesman/middleman has said. This provision is especially useful in a hire purchase or conditional sale
transaction.

Everything that has been said above is equally applicable to a
conditional sale agreement, except that if the goods are defective
then the statute which applies is the Sale of Goods Act.

Credit card transactions

3. Martin purchased a television set from Scurrys for £300 using
his Barcess credit card. His credit limit is £4,000. The card is of the
variety like Access and Visa. The television set breaks down after
two months.

When Martin returned to the store to complain he discovered they had gone into liquidation due to the recession. He settled his Barcess account in full at the end of last month. Martin has entered into a three party debtor-creditor-supplier agreement for restricted use running account credit. His contract with the store is governed by the Sale of Goods Act 1979 and there would appear to be a breach of the implied conditions as to merchantability and fitness of purpose. Normally this would entitle Martin to reject the goods and recover any monies paid, but this is of course subject to the doctrine of acceptance which could mean a damages only remedy. Obviously here there is no point in pursuing an action against the store as a judgement would prove worthless but there is a breach of contract.

Here, because there is a three party debtor-creditor-supplier agreement for restricted use credit, the cash price of the goods is between £100 and £30,000 and the agreement is regulated, section 75 of the C.C.A. comes into play. This is a vitally important provision:

(a) Section 75 only applies to three party debtor-creditor-supplier agreements. It does not apply to hire purchase, credit sale or conditional sale agreements.

(b) Section 75 only applies where the agreement is regulated (so your answer would clearly be different where the card was of the American Express or Diners Club variety as these are exempt agreements under the Act) and the cash price of the goods is between £100 and £30,000.

(c) Section 75 says that where the debtor has a claim in either contract or misrepresentation against the supplier he has a like claim against the creditor.

In this case therefore, Martin has a claim in contract against the creditors by virtue of a breach of the Sale of Goods Act, The price limits are satisfied. Martin can therefore use section 75 as a sword to recover the £300.

Note Also:

(a) Martin is free to pursue his action at any time against Barcess. The retailer does not have to have gone into liquidation, the retailer may just be unco-operative.

(b) The creditor is liable to the extent that the supplier would have been liable, not just for the amount of credit extended to the debtor, *e.g.* Martin could have used his credit card to leave a £50 deposit and paid the balance in cash. Barcess would still be liable for £300. (In a paper headed Joint Liability issued by the OFT (August 1991) this is the departmental view despite the card-issuers attempts to relieve themselves of liability.)

The television set could have exploded causing personal injuries to Martin. Martin could have sued Scurrys for the set and his injuries in contract. He could therefore sue the creditor for these amounts.

(c) Martin might not have settled his credit card account. Can he use section 75 as a shield to avoid payment? To date there is no English authority on the point, but in the Scottish case of *United Dominions Trust* v. *Taylor* 1980, Mr. Taylor purchased a car from a garage with the assistance of a loan from UDT. He had been passed on to UDT by the garage, so there was a connected lender three party debtor-creditor-supplier situation. Mr. Taylor paid nothing under the agreement, felt his car was a "heap of junk" and when the garage refused to do anything about it, he abandoned the car on the forecourt. UDT sued him for defaulting on the loan. Mr. Taylor used section 75 as a defence, claiming the money had been used to purchase defective goods and his claim was upheld by the courts. Although this decision has been attacked academically, from a consumer's point of view it seems a perfectly sensible solution. The case can be put forward as persuasive authority that section 75 can be used as a defence.

Loan linked agreements

4. Martin purchased a new car from News Garage Ltd. for £8,000 with the assistance of a loan of £6,000 from Grasping Finance Ltd. He had been passed on to the Finance Company by News Garage. With interest charges of £1,200 the total loan repayable was £7,200. Martin paid a £2,000 deposit to News Garage.

After three weeks the engine "seized up" and News Garage were only prepared to repair the car. In this case Martin's contract for the car is governed by the Sale of Goods Act 1979 and he would have all the usual rights for a breach of merchantable quality as outlined earlier. The problem of acceptance, as outlined in the case of *Bernstein* v. *Pamson Motors* 1987 must be considered, but, assuming no acceptance has occurred, then Martin could have a claim in contract against News Garage for £8,000 and interest charges incurred. Because of the loan he has entered into a three party debtor-creditor-supplier agreement for restricted use fixed sum credit. The cash price of the goods is between £100 and £30,000 and the agreement is regulated as it is credit of less than £15,000 to an individual and it is not exempt.

Section 75 therefore comes into play. Where the debtor has an action in contract, as here for £8,000+, he has a like claim against the creditor. This is *not* limited to the amount of the money he has borrowed, *i.e.* £6,000 but includes *any* contractual claim he may have against the supplier. Therefore, if Martin is having problems with the garage he could sue the finance company for the return of his £2,000 and resist a claim from the finance company by using section 75 as a defence. See *UDT* v. *Taylor* 1980.

It can be seen that it is therefore advantageous to use section 75 as a means of having another potential defendant to draw in when things go wrong. It is particularly useful to pay deposits using a credit card so that if the supplier company does go into liquidation the monies can be recovered from the credit card company.

Loan agreement

5. If Martin had gone to the bank for a loan to enable him to purchase the car, then again as in Example 1, his only remedy would be against the garage as it is a debtor-creditor agreement. He would remain liable to pay the loan.

6. A conditional sale agreement has been dealt with in (2). Thus, it can be seen that buying goods using a form of credit can be very useful to a consumer where defective goods are involved.

---

11. THE DEBTOR IS IN FINANCIAL DIFFICULTIES

The final set of examination questions arise from the situation where the debtor cannot afford his credit repayments. The creditor should, from a practical point of view, always be notified to see whether any accommodation can be reached before the situation reaches crisis point.

Naturally, the course of action to be taken does depend on whether the debtor wishes to keep the goods or to rid himself of them. Assuming the debtor wishes to rid himself of the goods, the cheap ways out of the agreement which were discussed earlier should be considered, *e.g.* lack of licence, cancellable agreements, etc., but if nothing can be done under these headings then a solution which inevitably will cost money may be found.

First, the type of credit agreement must be considered

   (a) If it is a loan then the overriding principle is that it has to be repaid. There is no way out for the debtor unless the goods are defective and it is a loan linked agreement. His only remedy will lie in the fact he may be given more time to pay and this will be explained later.

   (b) If it is a hire purchase or conditional sale agreement, then the finance company has legal title to the goods and one of the options open to a debtor who does not wish to keep the goods is to exercise his rights to terminate under sections 99–100 of the 1974 C.C.A.

Termination is a costly option and should be a last resort as it is expensive and the debtor ends up with nothing. For termination to operate under section 99:

   (a) The agreement must be regulated under the C.C.A.;
   (b) It is available at any time before the final payment falls due;
   (c) All arrears must be paid;
   (d) The debtor is liable to pay the creditor half of the total price.

Some examples will serve to illustrate these points.

Example 1

Gill buys a music system for a total price of £2,804 in November 1992. This figure includes a deposit of £500 and interest charges of £350. The balance is repayable by 24 payments of £96. Gill pays one instalment in December, then loses her job and falls into arrears. She visits you in April, now being three months in arrears. One of Gill's options is to terminate. As the total price is £2,804 the starting half point figure is £1,402. Gill has paid £596. This leaves a balance of £806 to pay *including the arrears*. Gill has to clear the arrears which total £288 but in section 100(3) there is a proviso that states if a case does come before the courts, then if the court is satisfied that a sum less than one half would be equal to the loss suffered by the creditor then it may order a lesser amount. Gill can try and argue that because the finance company is receiving almost new goods back quickly, paying them the arrears of £288 should satisfy them. She must be prepared however, to pay the full balance of £806 and hand the goods back. It can therefore be seen that termination is a costly option.

Remember always to check your total price figure; divide by two, all arrears must be cleared and the remaining balance, taking the figure to one half, must be reached. Negotiations can be tried on this remaining balance where the goods are relatively new, but the debtor must be advised of his potential liability to pay the full half figure.

Example 2

Cecil purchases a car on a conditional sale agreement for a total price of £12,500 including interest charges. He gives a £1,700 deposit, leaving the balance repayable by 36 monthly instalments of £300. After 15 months he loses his job and falls into arrears. He visits you for advice when he is two months in arrears. This time, the total price being £12,500, half equals £6,250. He has paid £1,700 plus £4,500 making a total of £6,200.

He only has to pay £50 to terminate, but owes £600 in arrears. If he therefore clears the arrears of £600 this will end his liability. Remember, all arrears have to be cleared.

Example 3

Jane has a hire purchase agreement on her washing machine for £600 including interest charges of £150. Jane pays a £120 deposit with the balance repayable over two years. After paying for three months she is unable to keep up the repayments. She visits you, being one payment in arrears. The total price is £600, half the total price equals £300. Jane has paid £180 and is therefore liable to pay a further £120 including the arrears. If she wishes to terminate, again she must clear the arrears but can attempt to negotiate on the balance, but must be warned of her liability to pay the full amount.

Example 4

If an installation charge is involved then the half figure which must be reached is the installation charge in full, plus half the remaining balance. Thus, in the example above, assume the £600 figure included a £30 installation charge and Jane again wishes to terminate. This time the half figure would be £600 minus £30= £570. Divide the remaining balance by two =£285, and add back the installation charge which brings the total to £315. Therefore, this time if Jane wishes to terminate she will have to find £135 instead of £120.

Where the debtor wishes to keep the goods

All of the above examples have been on the basis that the debtor wishes to get rid of the goods, but what of the debtor who wishes to hang on to the goods, despite being in financial difficulties.

Again, the advice depends on the type of credit agreement. If the agreement is a loan, either loan-linked or arranged independently, it must be repaid. The goods purchased are the debtor's and, if necessary, he can sell them to repay the loan. If a debtor under any kind of credit agreement gets into difficulties, then he will receive a default notice from the credit company under section 87 of the Act.

This notice must be served before the creditor can enforce his rights under the agreement. The default notice must say what the breach is, what must be done to remedy it, and give the debtor at least seven days to make it right, (C.C.A., ss.87 and 88). For our purposes here, once the debtor has received a default notice he can apply to court under section 129 for what is known as a time order.

What this does in effect is give the debtor more time to clear off his arrears so that if he wishes to keep his goods he should do this.

Normally time orders only relate to arrears so if the debtor has a loan he will have a longer time to pay (and obviously more interest charges!) but in the case of a hire purchase or conditional sale agreement the time order can relate to future payments (C.C.A., s.133), so that in effect the whole agreement has been rewritten.

Special help for debtors in a hire purchase and conditional sale agreement

Remember if the debtor has a hire purchase or conditional sale agreement he does not own the goods. The Finance Company is the owner. If the debtor wishes to retain the goods then one tactic he can try is to make the goods "protected." This means that the creditor will have to obtain a court order before the goods can be seized; inevitably this takes time and will give the debtor more time to try and get out of his financial difficulties.

Under section 90 of the Consumer Credit Act goods are protected:

(a) If the debtor has paid more than one third of the total price (*Note*: the difference between termination which is a half and protected goods which is one third). The same rules apply to calculating one third and installation charges, *i.e.* Joanna buys a cooker on hire purchase for £390 including a £30 installation charge and interest charges of £50. One third $=(£390-£30$ divided by 3$)=£120$. The installation charge is then added back in, so if Joanna wanted to make the goods protected £150 would be the target figure.

(b) The debtor must be in breach (she would be as she is in arrears).

(c) The agreement must not have been terminated.

(d) The property must be in the creditor.

If the creditor does seize the goods back without a court order when more than one third has been paid, the agreement terminates and the debtor can recover all her payments (another case of the debtor having their cake and eating it!) (C.C.A. s.91).

Therefore one piece of advice which can be given to debtors is to try and make the goods protected.

However, it should also be noted that regardless of how little has been paid, if a creditor has to enter any premises he must obtain a court order, so in any event, as the cooker is on Joanna's premises, a court order would have to be obtained, (C.C.A., s.92). Protected goods provisions are therefore of most use in the case of motor vehicles left frequently parked on the roadside.

One last matter which ought to be taken into consideration is that section 173(3) of the Act says "where a court order or a validating order by the Director General is required, the consent of the debtor given at the time will be equally effective." Obviously there could be an issue of "true consent" and earlier cases on older credit legislation have considered this but clearly a consumer who wishes to retain his goods should not be advised to hand them back.

Extortionate credit bargains

Finally, in the context of "I can't afford to pay," the issue of extortionate credit bargains under sections 137–140 must be considered. This is a new concept, introduced by the Act in 1978 but is currently being reviewed by the Office of Fair Trading and new legislation could be enacted in the near future.

The extortionate credit bargain provisions in the Act are unusual in that:

(a) they apply even if the credit exceeds £15,000. The only criteria is that the debtor should be an individual.

and

(b) if the agreement is exempt.

What bargains are extortionate?

Section 138 states that a bargain is extortionate if it requires the debtor to make payments which are grossly exorbitant or otherwise grossly contravene ordinary principles of fair dealing.

A *non-exhaustive* list of relevant factors is then set out. These include *inter alia*:

(a) Prevailing interest rates at the time the bargain was made;
(b) factors affecting *the debtor, e.g.* age, health, business capacity. (Questions in this area often involve John, an elderly pensioner – who signed a credit agreement with an APR of 100 per cent.)
(c) factors *affecting the creditor* such as his relationship with the debtor and the degree of risk undertaken.

The debtor can take proceedings through the County Court to have the bargain reopened. Section 171(7) provides that if the debtor alleges the bargain is extortionate, the onus is on the creditor to prove that it is not, *e.g. Bank of Baroda* v. *Shah* 1988.

If the court decides the bargain is extortionate, it can re-write the agreement. Every case will depend on its own facts. See *e.g. Ketley* v. *Scott* 1981, *Davies* v. *Direct Loans* 1986.

The debtor with surplus funds

So far we have considered the debtor who is in financial difficulties. To finish this section – what about the debtor who wishes to repay a credit agreement early because he has a surplus of funds. Under section 94 there is a non-excludable right to do this. The debtor will *not* receive a rebate on the *full* amount of interest but will receive some rebate using the appropriate tables (C.C.A., s.95).

Lost credit cards

This is governed by section 84 of the C.C.A. The debtor should notify the Card Company immediately of the loss by telephone. This must usually be confirmed in writing. The debtor remains liable for the first £50 if the card is misused prior to notification so the faster the credit card company is notified, the better. If the debtor gave the card to a third party and the card was misused, the debtor remains liable without limit.

---

12. ESCAPING FROM CASH AGREEMENTS

In the section on credit agreements we have seen that there is an escape route for someone buying under a cancellable credit agreement.

WHAT IF CASH IS EMPLOYED AS THE METHOD OF PAYMENT?

The Consumer Protection (Cancellation of Contracts concluded away from Business Premises) Regulations 1987 may assist a consumer. These regulations have been enacted pursuant to a European Directive in an attempt to standardise liability throughout the European Community.

The Regulations provide for a seven day cooling-off period, during which agreements covered by the Regulations can be cancelled by the customer without penalty. Traders are required to give their customers written notice of the right of cancellation and the name and address of a person against whom it can be exercised. If this is not done, the agreement will be void and unenforceable against the customer.

Contracts covered.

Where goods and services cost more than £35 and the contract results from an *unsolicited visit* by the trader to the customer's home or place of work (unsolicited means a visit which does not take place at the *express request* of the customer, *i.e.* a visit which has not clearly been initiated by the customer).

Note, this includes a visit which results from an unsolicited telephone call by a trader, during which an appointment is agreed.

There are a number of exempted contracts, *e.g.* the construction of buildings, but agreements for the repair or improvement of property are covered. The Department of Trade and Industry have published useful information on this legislation in their leaflet "Selling Away from Business Premises."

How does the customer exercise his right of cancellation?

By serving written notice on the trader during the time within the cooling-off period.

Contracting out

Any attempt to contract out of the regulations is void.

---

13. CONSUMER HIRE AGREEMENTS

As well as covering credit agreements the Consumer Credit Act also covers hire agreements (C.C.A., s.15). It is intended in this chapter to highlight problems relating to hired goods.

In this time of recession some retail organisations have reported a large increase in consumers turning to hire goods as compared to buying them. Rumbelows report a large increase in the hiring sector, as more consumers work out it may be cheaper for them to rent a washing machine for, say, £16 a month, and have all their repair bills covered and a prompt call out service.

Of course, if the goods are defective or do not match their description, etc., there is no breach of the Sale of Goods Act as there has been no transfer of property. Hire goods are caught by Part I of the 1982 Supply of Goods and Services Act (ss.7–9). Exclusion notices are caught by section 7 of the U.C.T.A. if there is an attempt to exclude liability for description, fitness for purpose of merchantable quality.

Hire agreements are caught by the Act if:

(a) there is a bailment of goods;
(b) by one person (the owner);
(c) to an individual;
(d) which is not hire purchase; and
(e) which is capable of lasting for more than three months; and
(f) does not require the hirer to pay more than £15,000.

Therefore agreements such as those for washing machines, videos, satellite dishes and televisions all come within the ambit of the Act.

Termination of the Agreement

This is governed by section 101 of the Act. This gives a statutory right to the hirer to terminate it after 18 months, even if the hiring was for a fixed term of a longer period. (Obviously, if the hirer can terminate under the actual agreement before 18 months this will take priority.)

Termination only operates for the future and sums which have accrued due must be paid. The hirer must give a termination notice which is equivalent to the shortest payment interval, or three months, whichever is less. So, if the washing machine was on a two year rental with payments every two months, the hirer could give notice to terminate at the end of month 16.

There are some exemptions in section 101(7), but these relate mainly to commercial equipment.

14. THE TRADE DESCRIPTIONS ACT

In earlier chapters the civil law relating to the consumer has been considered. The following chapters on Pricing, Unsafe Goods, Food Safety and Trade Descriptions, involve criminal liability and how the intervention of the criminal law can assist the consumer.

It will be noted that the description of goods is a great influencing factor on what persuades consumers to buy goods. If the description is wrong, then there can be a breach of section 13 or a possible action in misrepresentation. The incorrect description can also give rise to criminal liability under 1968 Trade Descriptions Act.

If a conviction is obtained under the Act, then under the powers of the Criminal Court Act 1973 (as amended) compensation of up to £5,000 per offence can be obtained for the consumer.

Using the Act could therefore be a cheaper, easier way of obtaining compensation than taking a claim before the civil courts.

Basic requirements of the Act

The Act operates in two areas:

(a) In relation to goods;
(b) in relation to services.

Goods

Section 1(1) says any person who in the course of a trade or business:

(a) applies a false trade description to any goods; or
(b) supplies or offers to supply any goods to which a false trade description is applied shall be guilty of an offence.

Section 1 is a strict liability offence, *i.e.* no *mens rea* is required.

Section 2 sets out a list of 10 ways in which a trade description can be applied, *e.g.* if a can is described as containing 200 grams and only 50 grams are inside, there would be a breach of section 2(1)(a).

If a sweater is described as 100 per cent wool and it is in fact 50 per cent acrylic and 50 per cent cotton there would be a breach of section 2(1)(c).

The most common offences are committed in relation to the "clocking" of cars. Car complaints form the largest part of the complaints dealt with by the Office of Fair Trading (see OFT Annual Report 1993) and lead to more convictions and compensation orders being made than in any other area. Turning back the milometer on cars is capable of being a false trade description under section 2(1)(j), *R.* v. *Hammerton Cars Ltd.* 1976.

Punishment

Although most convictions result in a fine (the maximum for summary conviction is £5,000) recent cases have made it clear, particularly in the clocking cases as outlined above, that car dealers who persistently clock cars could find themselves subject to a prison sentence, *R.* v. *Hewitt, The Times,* June 1991.

Acting in the course of a business

The offence is only committed by someone acting in the course of a business. Private individuals are not normally "caught" by the Act, (but see section 23, the by-pass provision which could result in a conviction).

"In the course of a business" was considered in the case of *Davies* v. *Sumner* (1984 H.L.) where a self-employed courier part-exchanged his car which had an oedometer reading of 18,100 when it had in fact covered 118,000. When the defendant sold the car to the garage, was he acting in the course of a trade or business? The House of Lords decided not, as the sale was not an *integral* part of the business (the defendant was not in the car business, previously he had leased cars and was not involved in a regular practice of exchanging cars). It was merely incidental to the carrying on of the business. Students will note that this was the same view taken in the case of *R.* v. *B Customs Brokers* v. *U.D.T.* 1988.

In *Devlin* v. *Hall* (*The Times,* June 6, 1990) the *first sale* by a proprietor of a taxi firm of one of his two cars could not be said to amount to a normal regular practice and was therefore not done in the course of a business.

On the other hand in *Havering London Borough* v. *Stevenson* 1970, the defendant ran a car-hire business but intermittently sold cars from the forecourt. Although this was not his main business, and he was not a car dealer, the courts held he was acting in the course of a business as there was a practice of selling off cars.

Note: the Act applies to an offer to supply, *section 6* and not just where the goods have actually been supplied. This covers the invitation to treat point in *Pharmaceutical Society of Great Britain* v. *Boots Cash Chemists* 1952.

What about disclaimer notices?

What better way to avoid liability than to try and disclaim. Can this be done under the Act?

This device has been used particularly in the car clocking cases. It can be effective, but is subject to many restrictions:

In order to be effective, the disclaimer must be introduced before the trader supplies the goods. In *Norman* v. *Bennett* 1974, it was stated that "the disclaimer must be as bold, precise and compelling as the trade description itself and must equal the trade description in the extent to which it is likely to get home to anyone interested in receiving the goods." In other words, the milometer reading has to be made meaningless.

Sentences in small print will not protect dealers, and general notices would appear to be ineffective.

See *Zawadski* v. *Sleigh* 1975; *London Borough of Waltham* v. *T.G. Wheatley* 1978.

Note: the difference between a car dealer who sells a "clocked" car and one who actually clocks the car himself.

Newman v. *Hackney* 1982 states that if the dealer is found to have clocked the car himself, then the disclaimer doctrine is not available.

The doctrine is therefore only available to someone who has *not* clocked the car.

There is a Code of Practice for Motor Dealers. No particular form of disclaimer is used, but paragraphs 3.8 and 3.9 state:

(a) The need to verify the recorded mileage with previous owners;
(b) that any disclaimer used must be as bold and precise and compelling as the car's mileage reading itself and as effectively brought to the prospective customer's attention.

To date, despite many moves made by consumer associations to have the mileage information recorded on the vehicle registration document, no legislation has been enacted in this area.

Disclaimers in other areas

The recent case of *R.* v. *Price* 1993 has raised problems for Trading Standards Officers in relation to counterfeit goods. A market trader put a notice on his stall saying "brand copies." He was selling T-shirts bearing brand names like "Levi" and "Adidas." The Divisional Court agreed this disclaimer was sufficient to escape conviction under the Trade Descriptions Act. Trading Standards Departments have expressed great concern at this case (see ITSA Press Release MPW/EDD/180693) but have said that although prosecutions will not work under the Trade Descriptions Act, they will use other legislation, *e.g.* Trade Marks Act 1938 or Copyright Designs and Patents Act 1988 to obtain a conviction. In *Lewin* v. *Fuell* 1991 the Divisional Court had to consider whether an oral disclaimer in relation to watches, which were offered for supply bearing names such as "Cartier" and "Rolex" could be effective in nullifying the false trade descriptions. The Court ruled that the offence was committed when the goods were exposed for supply and as the disclaimer came after the offence had been committed it was too late to be effective.

Although defences will be discussed later, it is worth noting one particular detail at this point in relation to disclaimers. One defence under section 24 is that the defendant had taken all reasonable precautions and exercised all due diligence to avoid the commission of an offence. In *Simmons* v. *Potter* 1975 it was held that because the defendant car dealers had not used a disclaimer notice, they had not exercised all reasonable precautions. They were therefore guilty of an offence. See also *Lewin* v. *Fuell* 1991.

15. SERVICES

Section 14 of the Trade Descriptions Act relates to services. The difference between section 1 relating to goods and section 14 is that an element of *mens rea* is required. Section 14 states:

> It shall be an offence for any person *in the course of any trade or business* (so what was said in relation to *section 1* applies here) to make a statement which *he knows* to be false or *recklessly* to make a statement which is false as to services, accommodation or facilities.

This section will be considered with particular reference to holidays. These are the most likely kinds of service to occur in examinations and the most common service complaint to arise in practice. For a recent holiday case see *West Yorkshire Trading Standards Service* v. *Eurosites plc* 1993.

Points to note:

1. *Mens rea* is required, *MFI Warehouses* v. *Nattrass* 1973; *Wings Ltd.* v. *Ellis* 1984. Trading Standards Department in Mid-Glamorgan has decided against attempting a prosecution against Hoover plc as a result of the complaints arising from their recent free flights offer (September 1993 Press Release) on the basis of the difficulties of proving recklessness or intention on the part of the company and the problems relating to future promises (see below). To date

Hoover has acknowledged many civil cases are pending against them.

2. A statement of intention relating to a *future* promise which is unfulfilled will not be a false trade description, *Beckett* v. *Cohen* (1973) 1 A.E. 720. Therefore artists' impressions of hotels in holiday brochures, stating the hotel "will be open in time for the next summer season" or "will have. . . . " will not give rise to successful actions under the Act. (Although there may be liability under the civil law.)

3. *Note*: however, if the description *implies* the *facility is in existence* then it may be actionable, *R.* v. *Clarksons Holidays* 1972. If the promise can be construed as an implied statement of *present* intention again a conviction may be obtained, *e.g. British Airways* v. *Taylor* 1974 (Airline overbooking); *R.* v. *Avro plc* (tickets issued by flight-only operator, the return flight did not exist).

4. If the facility existed at the moment the statement was made, but has broken down subsequently, then there will not normally be liability under the Act, *Sunair* v. *Dodds* 1970.

So that, if a hotel is advertised as having air-conditioning or satellite TV and this breaks down whilst the consumer is at the hotel, there will be no liability under the Trade Descriptions Act (although again there may be liability under the civil law).

5. What if the facility has never existed at all?

Wings v. *Ellis* 1984. The Respondents published a brochure which *inter alia* gave details of a holiday hotel in Sri Lanka. The hotel was stated as being fully air conditioned. The hotel did in fact have no air conditioning. The second edition of the tour brochure corrected the error and instructions were given out to travel agents. Mr. X obtained a first edition of the brochure, was never given the correct information and booked the holiday. Wings were charged under section 14(1)(a) and were convicted. Although they had no desire to mislead the consumer, the simple question to be asked was did they know the statement was false at the time when it was made and the clear answer to this was yes, with reference to the *mens rea* required. See also *R.* v. *Avro plc* 1993.

6. The Act can give rise to multiple prosecutions as an offence can be committed every time the description is published, (*R.* v. *Thomson Holidays Ltd.* 1974).

7. What if the Defendant tries to make matters right?

Can this "cancel" out the offence?

Cowburn v. *Focus* 1983. Here, the defendant company ran a promotional offer, stating that 20 films could be hired free when a consumer rented a TV. This offer in fact expired on November 9, 1981 but the offer placards remained prominently displayed in the shop window. This offer had been replaced by an offer for six free films. When the consumer rented the TV set on November 12 he was given a voucher for 6 free films and was asked for £1.50 towards postage and packing. As soon as he complained he was sent a refund of £1.50 and a voucher for 20 films. However, Trading Standards prosecuted and a successful conviction was obtained.

HOLIDAYS

At this stage, before we leave trade descriptions, in the light of the fact that holiday questions crop up with regularity in Consumer law examinations, it is worth noting certain matters:

1. In every holiday question look and see whether there is possible liability under the Trade Descriptions Act 1968. This could result in a compensation order for the aggrieved individual without the necessity of pursuing individual civil actions.

2. 1992 saw the introduction of the Package Travel Package Holidays and Package Tours Regulations 1992. These regulations result from European Directive 90/314/EEC and are enacted under Statutory Instrument 3288.

The regulations create both civil and criminal liability and apply to packages sold in the U.K. on or after December 31, 1992. Basically, a qualifying package must have been pre-arranged at an inclusive price and cover over 24 hours or include overnight accommodation. Regulation 2 contains definitions and refers to terms such as organiser and retailer rather than tour operator and travel agent. Business and conference travel could be covered under the regulations as the definition of consumer is wide enough to embrace them.

Regulation 4 creates implied terms for civil liability. Package organisers or retailers shall not supply any descriptive matter concerning the package which misleads the consumer. If they do, they will be liable to compensate the consumer for any loss which the consumer suffers in consequence. Other regulations set out what information should be given to consumers before the contract is concluded and before the package commences. Included in Regulation 15 is a term that the organiser and/or retailer should be strictly liable for the proper performance of the obligations under the contract whether or not they are providing the service or whether such services are to be provided by other suppliers. There are also terms involving security for refunds of money and for repatriation of the consumer in the event of insolvency.

The Department of Trade and Industry have published an 18 page Guidance Leaflet to the Regulations which students will find most useful. It should be noted that the Regulations do *not* replace existing law. To date there are no reported cases in either the civil or criminal law area.

3. When a consumer books a holiday on behalf of himself and his family it does appear that, contractually, any aggrieved party member may sue on the basis of agency, (*Jackson* v. *Horizon Holidays* 1975). This doctrine still appears to be true as far as holidays are concerned, in spite of what was said in *Woodar Investment Development Ltd.* v. *Wimpey Construction* 1980.

4. Under the civil law a holiday is a service. It cannot be split into component parts, so if something goes wrong it will give rise to:

(a) a breach of section 13 of the Supply of Goods and Services Act, (*Best* v. *Wilson Travel* 1993) or, more likely;

(b) a breach of contract, as an express term has been breached (consumers generally book with very precise terms as regards holiday accommodation so it is easier to sue for a breach of express terms);

(c) an action in misrepresentation;

(d) an action using the 1992 Regulations set out above.

5. Damages for distress and disappointment are often awarded in holiday cases. Again, this doctrine appears to have survived in the holiday cases despite the more restrictive approach taken in *Hayes* v. *Dodd* 1990. In the leading case of *Jarvis* v. *Swan Tours* 1973, the total cost of the holiday was £63.45. The holiday was a disaster and the amount awarded, including distress and disappointment was £125.

6. In order to gain maximum benefit from the special damages rules in *Hadley* v. *Baxendale*, if there is a special request or problem, make sure the consumer notes this in writing to the tour operator. In *Kemp* v. *Intasun* (1987) a casual conversation with the travel agent, by a consumer regarding her husband's asthmatic condition, did not have contractual consequences for the operator.

7. As well as pursuing civil actions through the courts, a consumer may instead decide to pursue the claim via arbitration through ABTA (The Association of British Travel Agents). There is no mandatory obligation placed on the consumer to use this service, but it is an option to be considered. The case is heard on a documents only basis, with none of the parties appearing to argue the case.

8. Legislation has also been enacted in relation to Timeshares. This is another area which has given rise to many complaints to the OFT. Amongst its sections, the 1992 Act contains provisions for a cooling-off period of 14 days for potential time-sharers, but this right is only of use to those consumers buying in the U.K. or

where the transaction is governed by English law. Failure to comply could result in a fine of up to £5,000 on summary conviction. A timeshare buyer who cancels a timeshare agreement within the cooling-off period will be entitled to claim back any advance payments and no cancellation fee can be made. The problem of Timeshares in, *e.g.* Tenerife and the Algarve has yet to be resolved, although a European Directive is expected in the not too distant future.

Defences to a Trade Descriptions Act claim

To return to trade descriptions, some defences will now be considered, it should be noted that the due diligence defence is also of relevance in relation to food safety, misleading prices and product liability. Some principles of general application are set out below.

Section 24 of the Trade Descriptions Act states:

It shall be a defence for the person charged to prove

(a) that the commission of the offence was due to a mistake, or to reliance on information supplied to him, or to the act or default of another person, an accident, or some other cause beyond his control; and

(b) that he took all reasonable precautions and exercised all due diligence to avoid the commission of such an offence by himself or any person under his control.

Cars and the disclaimer doctrine have been considered earlier, but it should be noted that an oral disclaimer would not be a defence under section 24 as reasonable precautions would at least have included a written disclaimer alongside the false trade description *Lewin* v. *Fuell* 1991.

The various parts in (a) are separate and distinct, *e.g.* if mistake is pleaded, the mistake must be of the person charged, and no-one else. A corporate offender will *not* be able to rely on the mistake of one of its employees, *Birkenhead and District Co-operative Society* v. *Roberts* 1970.

Act or default of another person

The case of *Tesco Supermarkets* v. *Nattrass* 1972 which has caused immense difficulties in practice, established that insofar as a company is concerned, its employees are "another person," allowing the defence of act or default of another person to be successfully pleaded. Only executive members for example, a Director, will be classed as the company. However, both limbs must be satisfied, so in *Haringey & Piro Shoes* 1976 although the offence was due to the act or default of another, not all reasonable precautions nor all due diligence had been exercised.

Sampling and Testing in relation to due Diligence

Can suppliers dealing with large quantities of goods rely on sampling to show they have exercised all due diligence and taken all reasonable precautions? This is a difficult area and every case will have to be decided on a question of fact, but in *Rotherham Metropolitan B.C.* v. *Raysun (U.K.) Ltd.* 1988 the defendants imported 100,000 packets of children's crayons per annum. The Hong Kong agents were supposed to analyse samples and send back any adverse reports. None were ever received. A single packet was tested in England. The crayons were described as poisonless, whereas they contained an excessive amount of toxic material. The defendants were convicted as they had not taken all reasonable precautions. See *Hurley* v. *Martinez and Co. Ltd.* 1991 (supplier again acting on assurances given further up the chain of supply without independent verification). *Held* the Defence was   made out. In *P. & M. Supplies Essex Ltd.* v. *Devon County Council* 1991 the Divisional Court said that the burden was on the defendants themselves to show that their testing system was adequate for both the type and number of goods involved and that this system was carried out scrupulously. Again on the facts the defence was not made out. See also *Dudley Metropolitan Council* v. *Roy Firman Ltd* 1992.

16. UNSAFE GOODS

When the consumer has a contract, there are rights under section 14 of the Sale of Goods Act or equivalent statutes against the retailer and under the Consumer Protection Act against the manufacturer. Where there is no contract at all, the consumer will still have rights under the Consumer Protection Act.

In this chapter criminal liability for unsafe goods will be considered. The Department of Trade and Industry have for many years operated a Consumer Safety Unit. The statistics on injuries caused by defective products prove grim reading at times and the statute now governing criminal liability (replacing various consumer safety statutes) is the Consumer Protection Act 1987, P. II.

This creates a new concept of a general safety requirement for goods, *note*: The Act is *not* aimed at shoddy goods, it is aimed at *unsafe* goods and came into force on October 1, 1987. The Act therefore:

(a) Sets out a general offence of supplying consumer goods which are not reasonably safe;
(b) provides for safety regulations to be made for products;
(c) provides for a system of notices, *e.g.* prohibition and suspension, to assist Trading Standards Officers to enforce the Act.

The safety of a range of consumer goods continues to be controlled by regulations setting out in detail how certain types of goods must be made and what warnings and instructions should accompany them. The reasoning behind the Act is that it is *not* practical to make regulations for every product and the concept of the general safety requirement therefore closes a gap in the safety legislation.

Section 19 of the Act attempts to define what is safe, and states "safe in relation to any goods means that there is no risk or no risk apart from one reduced to a minimum," in other words, goods do not have to be 100 per cent. safe, but the risk factor must be reduced to a minimum.

Warnings and labels on goods must be considered, *e.g.* solvents; but it is important to note that under section 45 and section 11 certain goods are excluded from the safety regulations, *i.e. inter alia* crops, water, food, controlled drugs, medicinal products, aircraft, motor vehicles and tobacco. Although of course these may well be covered under other criminal statutes, *e.g.* Food Safety Act 1990.

The offence

Section 10(1) says a person shall be guilty of an offence if he:

(a) supplies any *consumer* goods which fail to comply with the general safety requirement;
(b) offers or agrees to supply any such goods; or
(c) exposes or possesses any such goods for supply.

(b) and (c) are included to avoid problems set out in *Pharmaceutical Society of Great Britain* v. *Boots Cash Chemists* 1952 involving mere invitations to treat. Also note that no injury needs to have been suffered for an offence to be committed.

Section 10(2) contains a non-exhaustive list of factors to be taken into account, including marketing and safety standards "published by *any* person" about the goods and also as in civil liability under the Consumer Protection Act, a cost/benefit discussion to determine how much it would cost in commercial terms to make the goods "safe" and whether consumers would be willing to pay this price.

The defences

Five important defences are set out in section 10(4) apart from the general due diligence ones:

(a) the goods conform in a relevant respect with a European Community obligation;

(b) the goods conform to any applicable safety regulations or safety standards set out by the Secretary of State for Trade and Industry for the purpose of the general safety requirement;

(c) that the "offenders" reasonably believed the goods would not be used or consumed in the United Kingdom. (In order that British exporters are not disadvantaged);

(d) that the goods were supplied in the course of a business and that at the time the retailer did not know or had no reasonable grounds for believing that the goods failed to comply with the general safety requirement. This is known as the retailers' defence but it will only work if the "offender" reasonably believed the goods to be safe;

(e) that the goods were not supplied as new, *i.e.* the general safety requirement does not apply to the sale of second-hand goods.

Enforcement powers

Section 11 contains the regulation power and states that regulations may be made not only about the goods, but also about information supplied with them or about them. The section also gives the power to place a permanent ban on unsafe products. Obviously this can take time. Accordingly there is an expedited procedure set out in section 11.

In section 14 the Act contains various measures by means of notices to stop the spread of unsafe goods. A suspension notice can be served on an individual trader (this prevents him disposing of his stock) or a prohibition notice. Sometimes of course the goods have actually reached the public, it is now possible for a notice to warn to be served on an individual trader requesting him to publish a warning about unsafe goods. Obviously manufacturers may still put out warnings and this is the way the public usually receive information of this kind. As far as getting traders and manufacturers to recall products, one of the gaps in this legislation is that there is no recall power. The newspapers are of course full of recalls from manufacturers regarding defective products, in an attempt to avoid civil liability.

As far as penalties are concerned, the offender can be subject to a maximum fine of up to £5,000 and up to six months imprisonment.

In the Guide to the 1987 Consumer Protection Act, published by the Department of Trade and Industry, businesses are given advice as to how to fulfil their obligations under the Act and encouragement is given to attain BS5750 on quality assurance, whereby companies can "establish document and maintain an effective and economic system for developing and maintaining the quality of their products."

Like product liability, adequate insurance cover is essential as is the necessity for good suppliers and good indemnity clauses between contracting parties.

The European position

There is proposed a General Product Safety Directive to standardise the safety of goods throughout Europe. This Directive was to have been implemented as far back as 1991, but has still not reached the statute books. At the time of writing the DTI anticipates that implementation will occur during the latter part of 1994.

---

17. FOOD SAFETY

In recent years there has been a massive increase in reported cases involving food poisoning. According to figures put out by the Department of Environmental Health, the number is steadily rising year by year.

In 1990 the Food Safety Act came into being, its aim being "to control all aspects of food safety throughout the food distribution chain, from the plough to the plate."

It should be noted that breaches of the Food Safety Act give rise to criminal liability (remember under the Sale of Goods Act an injured person can sue for a breach of section 14 and add their injury claims on as a direct consequence of the breach).

On indictment there is an unlimited fine and/or imprisonment for a maximum of two years. On summary conviction there is an upper limit fine of £20,000 for breaches of section 7, section 8 and section 14. For other breaches there are fines of up to £5,000 and imprisonment for a maximum of up to six months.

There are four major offences which students should know and appreciate, apart from many others contained in the Act. These are the provisions contained in sections 7, 8, 14 and 15. First of all the definition of food should be noted. This is partly defined by section 1(1). A second list of items are excluded in section 1(2).

Included in the definition are:

(a) Drinks (including bottled mineral water), but *not* the supply of water to premises (governed by the Water Act). *Note*: that the supply of water to the tap is governed by the various Water Acts, but that once the water has left the tap it is regulated by the Food Safety Act.
(b) Additives (s.1(1)(b)).
(c) Chewing Gum.

There are also sections governing contact materials (*i.e.* crockery, cutlery, plastic wrapping, etc). Excluded are:

(a) live animals;
(b) animal foodstuffs;
(c) controlled drugs and medicines.

Rendering food injurious to health

Section 7 creates a specific offence of rendering food "injurious to health with the intent that it should be sold for human consumption."

According to section 7 the offence can be committed in four ways:

(a) section 7.1(a) – by adding any article or substance to the food;
(b) section 7.1(b) – by using any article or substance as an ingredient in the preparation of the food;
(c) section 7.1(c) – abstracting any constituent from the food; or
(d) section 7.1(d) – subjecting the food to any other process or treatment.

Section 3 of the Act states a presumption that if food commonly used for human consumption is sold, the sale is for human consumption.

There is one loophole left in section 7, *i.e.* that no offence is committed by someone who *fails* to subject food to a necessary process or treatment. However, a successful prosecution should be available under section 8.

Selling food not complying with food safety requirements

Section 8 creates a number of offences. It says:

"Any person who sells for human consumption or offers exposes or advertises for sale for such consumption or has in his possession for the purpose of such sale or of preparation for such sale any food which fails to comply with food safety requirements shall be guilty of an offence."

It should be noted that there is no general safety requirement in respect of food as there is in the case of goods under the Consumer Protection Act and at the present time the draft European Directive on General Product Safety does not apply to food.

The offence in section 8 can only be committed if:

(a) food is rendered injurious to health under section 7;
(b) it is unfit for human consumption; or
(c) it is so contaminated that it would not be reasonable to expect it to be used for human consumption. (Section 8(2).)

Under previous legislation it has been held that a person can be convicted of an offence of selling food, even though the end result substance sold is not food at all. What is necessary is that it should be sold *as food*.

In *Meah* v. *Roberts* 1978 the defendant mistakenly supplied caustic soda instead of lemonade. He was convicted of an offence.

Note: that the loophole mentioned earlier in relation to section 7 (*i.e.* a failure to do something) could result in an acquittal under section 8(2)(a) as there has been no offence committed, *but* if the failure results in the food being unfit for human consumption, then an offence will have been committed under section 8(2)(b), so failure to act can lead to a successful prosecution.

What is meant by unfit for human consumption?

It should be noted that food can be unfit for human consumption even if it poses no health hazard. *David Greig* v. *Goldfinch* 1961 – this involved a pork pie found to be developing black mould under the crust. This was discovered to be a harmless bacteria. However, the justices fortunately found that the food was unfit for human consumption.

There had been difficulties in earlier cases when extras had been found in food, *e.g.* string in a loaf of bread, *Turner* v. *Owen* (1956) 1 Q.B. 48 or metal in a cream bun (*J. Miller* v. *Battersea* 1956). Arguments had been successfully put forward that these extras did not make food unfit for human consumption. Nowadays, the defendants should merely be charged under section 8(2)(c), *i.e.* supplying contaminated food.

Foods which mislead consumers

Sections 14 and 15 of the Act will now be considered. Basically the aim of these sections is to prevent consumers from being misled and to try and make sure that they obtain food "of the appropriate nature, substance and quality demanded" (already students should be thinking of the civil law under Sale of Goods Act 1979, ss.13 and 14).

Section 14 of the Food Safety Act states that any person who sells to a purchaser's prejudice any food which is not of the nature or substance or quality demanded by the purchaser shall be guilty of an offence. Thus, anyone who sells goods which do not correspond with their description could be guilty of an offence under section 14. In *McDonalds Hamburgers* v. *Windle* (1987) C.L.R. 200 the product requested was Diet McDonalds cola. Ordinary cola was served. An offence was committed.

The section may also be used where regulations prescribe that certain products can only be sold as "mince," for example when they contain not more than a certain percentage of fat. When regulatory standards are set down, food must comply with these standards in order to be of the substance demanded, *e.g.* fish cakes under the Food Standards Fish Cakes Order 1950 mean that to describe goods as a fish cake the fish cake has to have a 35 per cent. minimum fish content.

Section 15 of the Act says any person who gives with any food sold by him . . . a label . . . which falsely describes the food or is likely to mislead as to the nature or substance or quality of the food shall be guilty of an offence.

Again, there could be an overlap between sections 14 and 15. *Note*: the wording is *"likely to mislead"* no-one need actually be misled.

Thus these are the sections most likely to occur in examination questions. The statute also contains many powers for Food Inspectors to inspect and seize food (ss.7, 8 and 9) and to issue notices including powers to close down premises. These questions are not usually examined in depth on Consumer Law papers, but students should examine their particular syllabus and revise accordingly and make use of the many detailed works now appearing in this area.

Defences

Like most consumer protection statutes, the Food Safety Act does provide defences in certain situations, notably the due diligence defence contained in section 21(1). This defence is discussed in more detail in relation to trade descriptions and, broadly speaking, most of the principles can be transferred to the Food Safety legislation. For further information in this area students should again consult the detailed Guides to the Act.

18. MISLEADING PRICES

For some decades now there has been legislation to try to curb misleading prices and bargain offers. See, for instance section 11 of 1968 Trade Descriptions Act.

There is nothing more galling, as far as a consumer is concerned, than to think they have grabbed a bargain – only to discover when they reach the cash desk that they are asked for extra money. From a civil point of view, all law students are of course familiar with the famous decision in *Pharmaceutical Society of Great Britain* v. *Boots Cash Chemists* 1952. When consumers take their goods to the checkouts they are merely making an offer to purchase. The store, when displaying the goods, is making an invitation to treat. So, when Mrs. Bloggs takes her £5 bargain blouse to the cash desk and is asked for £15, under the civil law there is nothing she can do. Her offer of £5 has been rejected.

Attempts to legislate in this area have been criticised and have not met with much success. The latest attempt to control prices is now contained in Part III of the Consumer Protection Act 1987. This replaces section 11 of the Trade Descriptions Act and the Price Marking (Bargain Offers) Orders 1979.

The criminal offence of misleading consumers

The Act makes it a criminal offence to give consumers a misleading price indication about goods, services, or accommodation (including the sale of new homes). However, the Act only creates a general offence, it empowers the Secretary of State to approve a Code of Practice setting out guidance for retailers as to the practices they ought to follow. The important factor to note is that the Act does *not* require a retailer to do as the Code states. As long as the price indication is not misleading, there will be no criminal offence. On the other hand, even if the Code is complied with, if the price is misleading then the retailer could be guilty of an offence, although this situation is extremely unlikely.

The important factor is therefore that it is only a Code. The retail industry is seeking to put its house in order by self-regulation and the Secretary of State has agreed to this state of affairs.

Misleading is defined in section 21 of the Act and covers indications about any conditions attached to a price, about future prices, price comparisons, as well as indications about the actual price the consumer will have to pay.

The Act is enforced by Local Trading Standards Officers. The Act provides for a defence of due diligence as in other consumer criminal statutes. Obviously, as stated earlier, failure to follow the Code may make it difficult to show this defence.

The following guidance, *inter alia*, is given to retailers in the Code:

Price comparisons

(a) Para 1.1.2 – says the higher price as well as the price the retailer intends to charge should always be stated. Therefore, £10 reduced to £5 is good, *but* sale price £6 is misleading.

(b) Para 1.2.1 – says that in any comparison between the present selling price and another price, the previous price as well as the new lower price should be stated. Thus, "Blouse – £10, our normal price £20" complies with the Code.

(c) Following on from section 11 of the Trade Descriptions Act, in Para 1.2.2 – the Code states the product should have been available to consumers for at least 28 consecutive days in the last 6 months and in the same shop where the reduced price is being offered. If not, then this should be made clear.
This is why notices are appearing in shops under the heading of Consumer Protection Act – "The goods sold below were previously offered at our Outer Hebrides Branch between 14–16 January at £50 – Price Today £10". If no notice had been put up, the £10 notice would have contravened the Code.

(d) Para 1.2.3 – general disclaimers should not be used but specific stores and prices should be referred to.

(e) Para 1.2.6 – in the Code it is stated that if a series of reductions is made then the highest price, the intervening price and the current selling price should be shown, *e.g.* £10, £5 NOW ONLY £2.50. A leading chain store advertises during the sale period:

"£25 now £2.50. During the last 3 weeks these goods have been subject to a series of reductions. Further details on these reductions can be obtained from our Head Office."

It is a matter of conjecture as to whether this would satisfy the Code. No prosecution has yet been taken.

Introductory offers

(a) Para 1.3.1 – states that an introductory offer should not be described as such *unless* it is intended to charge a higher price later.

(b) Para 1.3.2 – states that an introductory offer should not be allowed to run overlong, but does *not* state how long this period should be. The word reasonable is quoted.

(c) Para 1.3.4 – future increased prices can be quoted, *e.g.* "Our price now until 10 June – £180: After Sales Price – £250."

This has become a favourite with the furniture retailing industry.

Comparison with prices related to different circumstances

There are a number of guidelines here. Again the most common to be met in practice are:

(a) For goods in a totally different state, *e.g.* "price in a kit form £50, ready assembled £100";

(b) Reductions for pensioners on certain days. These must be expressed in such a way that consumers are not misled and the goods or services must be available at the higher price. See 1.4.3 and 1.4.4.

References to worth or value

(a) Para 1.8.1 – states do not compare prices with slogans such as worth or value. Price comparisons with another trader's actual prices are allowed, *e.g.* see current B & Q Superstores campaign and Texas Homecare which is attempting to comply with 1.5.1.

(b) The slogan "if you can buy for less we will refund the difference"

Para 1.5.2 – states do not make statements like this about your own brand products unless your offer applies to another trader's equivalent goods. In one of the most recent cases under the Act, *R. v. Warwickshire C.C. ex parte Johnson* 1993, a price pledge promise stating, "We will beat any TV Hi-Fi and Video price by £20 on the spot" was held to be misleading.

This case failed however as the prosecution had been brought against the store manager and should have been brought against the retail organisation concerned.

Actual price to the consumer

(a) Para 2.1 – This follows closely on from the Trade Descriptions Act and is the easiest to pursue in practice. The Act makes it an offence to indicate a price for goods or services which is lower than the one that actually applies, so that in the example given in the beginning of this Chapter, when Mrs Bloggs was asked for £15 for the blouse, a criminal offence may have been committed.

(b) Paras 2.2.1 – 2.2.7 – deal with extras such as delivery charges and postage and state these *must* be clearly advertised. Also all price indications to private consumers must include VAT.

Service charges in restaurants and holidays

These should be stated if they are non-optional, para. 2.2.10 and should be incorporated within the price wherever practicable.

(a) Para 2.2.11 – states that extra non-optional charges, *e.g.* cover charges, can be made but these must be drawn prominently to the consumer's attention.

Guidance is also given in Part 2 on holiday and travel prices, and ticket prices. The Code should be consulted for further information. In particular, a second offence is created, *i.e.* a price indication which is correct when given but which later becomes misleading (Consumer Protection Act, s.20(2)).

Defences

Section 39 creates a defence of due diligence similar to that set out in the Trade Descriptions Act. It states, "subject to the following provisions of this section, it shall be a defence for that person to show he took all reasonable steps, and exercised all due diligence to avoid committing the offence."

Note: however, unlike section 24 of the Trade Descriptions Act, the defendant does not have to show that the offence was due to a number of specific reasons although in practice it is likely that the defendant will bring forward similar evidence.

To date the Code is being closely monitored to see if the system of self-regulation is working in practice.

The price marking order 1991

This is made under the 1974 Prices Act and implements two European directives 88/314 and 88/315 concerning prices, one in relation to foods and the other in relation to non-food products. This states that the selling price and, in certain cases, the unit price of goods which may be for sale by retail must be indicated in writing. Guidance is given to retailers as to where the selling price should be shown. In the case of *Allen* v. *Redbridge London Borough*

Council 1993, a chemist who stocked a wide range of perfumes locked them away for security reasons in a large glass cabinet. Price labels were placed on the base or back of the boxes, and a prospective customer could only discover the price by enlisting the help of a sales assistant. The Divisional Court held that the Order was fully complied with, provided there was on the article, clearly stated by whatever means, or alongside it some indicator unmistakably referring to it, showing the price. There is no requirement for a retailer to put the price label on the front of an article or to place the goods in a part of the shop where they could actually be handled by a consumer. It is sufficient that help from an assistant allows the consumer to see the price. This decision clearly overrules the earlier case of *Essex County Council* v. *Debenhams plc* 1992.

There are proposals for amendments to be made to the Order and these are currently under discussion by the Department of Trade and Industry. See discussion paper issued in July 1993.

---

19. WAYS OF PURSUING RIGHTS

In a work of this kind, it is not possible to go through the civil court system to show how a disappointed consumer can pursue their rights. However, it should be noted that as a large number of consumer claims involve amounts of less than £1,000 and as the issue of legal costs deters many litigants from going to court, one way of keeping costs down to a minimum is to commence an action through the Small Claims section of the County Court where the amount claimed is below £1,000.

The advantages of this system are:

(a) The plaintiff (and the defendant) are not, save in exceptional circumstances, responsible for the losing sides legal costs. Each side remains liable for their own costs and litigants are encouraged to represent themselves in a speedier and more informal atmosphere.

(b) There are court costs on issuing a summons (the maximum amount is £60 at the time of writing). This cost is usually borne by the losing side.

(c) The case is heard using the arbitration system and in most County Courts before a District Judge.

(d) No legal aid is available for representation although initial free advice may be given under the Green Form Scheme if income limits are satisfied.

Many retailers also belong to Trade Associations, *e.g.* Society of Motor Manufacturers and Traders and the Association may give assistance to consumers. There are also Codes of Practice governing various industries, *e.g.* ABTA governing the travel industry. Again a consumer may choose to gain satisfaction using arbitration schemes operated by bodies such as ABTA rather than use the court system. Consumers cannot be forced to use an arbitration scheme as opposed to the court system (Consumer Arbitration Agreements Act 1988).

Other ways of achieving consumer satisfaction

Many of the matters considered above involved the consumer in ultimately using the court system to gain redress.

There are other ways of achieving consumer satisfaction which are considered below and although they may not gain individual personal satisfaction for an aggrieved consumer, the consumer at large may be protected.

Many consumers report their complaints to Local Trading Standards Departments. Detailed figures are passed onto the Office of Fair Trading in London. The 1973 Fair Trading Act (which created the office of the Director General of Fair Trading) enables the Director General to begin procedures to halt practices which are harmful to consumers and to pursue individual traders whom he believes have persisted in unfair trading.

Some illegal practices

Examples of practices declared illegal are the banning of certain void exemption clauses. This was done by the Consumer Transactions (Restrictions on Statements) Order 1976. Another practice declared illegal was that of traders purporting to advertise as private sellers to avoid the provisions of the Trade Descriptions Act 1968 and section 14 of the Sale of Goods Act 1979 as these provisions only apply to sales made in the course of a business.

The Business Advertisments (Disclosure) Order 1977 declares that all business sellers must make it clear in advertisements that they are traders otherwise a criminal offence may have been committed.

Assurances under the Fair Trading Act

Sections 34–42 of the Fair Trading Act give the Director General powers to act against someone who in the course of business continually acts in a way detrimental to the interests of consumers. The

Director General can request from the offender an assurance that he will abandon the conduct in question.

All assurances are published in the Annual report of the Office of Fair Trading. If the offender breaks his assurance, the Director General can take proceedings against him using the Restrictive Practices Court with imprisonment being a possible ultimate penalty.

Again note that none of the powers listed above will give an injured consumer individual redress but the aim is to protect the public at large from unscrupulous traders.

20. CHECK LIST FOR CONSUMER LAW EXAMINATION

1. State which statute governs the transaction. This may be either:

(a) 1979 Sale of Goods Act; or
(b) 1973 Supply of Goods (Implied Terms) Act for Hire Purchase transactions;
(c) 1982 Supply of Goods and Services Act for work and materials contracts, exchange contracts, hire contracts and services contracts.

2. State the implied conditions which govern the contract, *i.e.* section 13 and section 14 of 1979 Sale of Goods Act and their equivalents in the 1973 and 1982 Act. Also relevant here is section 13 of 1982 Supply of Goods and Service Act as regards services.

3. Look at the effect of breach of condition.

4. Is there an exclusion clause?

5. Has it been incorporated into the contract by the common law rules?

6. If it has been incorporated, look at the effect of U.C.T.A. 1977 on the clause.

7. This will involve a discussion of section 6 and 7 of U.C.T.A. (where implied conditions *re* goods are excluded), and a discussion of the phrase "dealing as a consumer."

8. Where an attempt to exclude liability for services is made, this will involve a discussion of section 2 of U.C.T.A. and where property damage only is concerned, then a discussion of the reasonableness test is required.

9. All other exclusion clauses will be discussed under section 3 of Unfair Contract Terms and again the reasonableness test must be discussed.

10. Look at the effect of acceptance if it is a Sale of Goods Act contract, and affirmation if it is a 1973 or 1982 Act transaction.

11. Look at the remedies for breach of contract and the rule in *Hadley* v. *Baxendale*.

12. Consider the credit aspects.

13. State the basics of the C.C.A. 1974.

14. State clearly whether the transaction is hire purchase, conditional sale, loan, credit sale, credit card transaction, etc.

15. If the transaction is one of hire purchase or conditional sale, then aside from the defective goods aspect, termination under sections 99–101 of the C.C.A. 1974 will probably occur in the question.

16. If it is a loan, then state whether it is a debtor-creditor or debtor-creditor-supplier agreement, giving reasons. If it is a three party debtor-creditor-supplier agreement, then almost certainly a discussion of section 75 of the C.C.A. on joint liability is required.

17. Remember loan agreements cannot be terminated.

18. All aspects of credit should be looked at under three headings:

   (a) How can I get out of the agreement?

   (b) The goods are defective;

   (c) The debtor cannot afford to pay.

19. For questions involving 18(a), learn formalities licensing, cancellation, withdrawal and termination.

20. For questions involving 18(b), learn three basic statutes (*i.e.* 1979, 1973 and 1982 Acts) and section 75 and section 56 of the C.C.A. 1974.

21. For questions involving 18(c), learn extortionate credit, termination (if H.P. or conditional sale of agreement), and time orders.

22. Learn practically how to enforce the rights.

23. Always respond to the facts of the question, *e.g.* if a default notice has been sent respond to it, do not merely write out normal remedies.

24. Learn small claims and county court procedure.

25. Other advice, such as contacting trade associations, manufacturers (note 1987 Consumer Protection Act).

26. Arbitration – Compensation under 1968 Trade Descriptions Act.

21. SAMPLE QUESTIONS AND MODEL ANSWERS

Question 1

Alan purchased a Seal car nine months ago from Wonder-Cars Ltd. on hire purchase terms, financed by Grasping Finance Ltd. for a total price of £12,800 including charges of £2,500 and a part exchange allowance of £2,000. The price was payable over three years in equal instalments. During the negotiations, Wonder-Car's Sales Manager stated that Seal were noted for their mechanical reliability and finish. However, the brakes, gear box and body work were defective on delivery. Alan returned the car a dozen times to the garage during the nine months, but the faults were never corrected.

  (a) Advise Alan as to his rights and against whom they should be purchased.
  (b) Advise Alan as to the options open to him if he calls twelve months after the purchase and tells you that he has been made redundant, cannot afford the repayments and is three months in arrears. Assume that there are no faults this time.

Answer

The first part of this question is involved in identifying the type of transaction concerned. Once this has been done then the contractual rights will be analysed and Alan can be advised as to his rights and remedies.

Alan has purchased his car on hire-purchase terms. The transaction is therefore governed by Supply of Goods (Implied Terms) Act 1973. As the transaction is one of hire-purchase, Wonder-Cars will have sold the car to Grasping Finance Ltd. who will hire the car out to Alan with an option to purchase. Contractually Wonder-Cars "drop" out of the situation, and all of Alan's rights under the 1973 Act are exercisable against Grasping Finance Ltd.

Under the Act by section 10 where a person deals in the course of a business (as Grasping Finance do here) then there is an implied condition that:

a) The goods will be of merchantable quality.

Merchantable quality has the same meaning as stated in Sale of Goods Act 1979, s.14(6). We are told that the brakes, gear box and bodywork were defective on delivery and that the faults still remain.

It must be considered what a buyer's expectations are in relation to a new car. Clearly the car must work mechanically but what about appearance defects. In *Rogers* v. *Parish* 1985 the Court of Appeal said that a buyer not only expected a new car to function properly but that it should "look good." In *Bernstein* v. *Pamson Motors* 1986 the engine of a new Nissan car seized up. The car was said not to be of merchantable quality. The faults would seem to be sufficiently serious to say that this condition has there been breached.

Section 10 also states that the goods have to be reasonably fit for their purpose where the buyer relies on the skill and judgement of the seller. Where the buyer has "bought" from a reputable supplier, as here, then reliance can be implied, *Grant* v. *Australian Knitting Mills* 1936. Clearly it can be argued that a car which keeps breaking down is unfit for its purpose *R.* v. *B. Customs Brokers* v. *U.D.T.* 1987 and therefore there is a breach of this implied condition.

Section 9 of the 1973 Act states that the goods must comply with their description. The sales manager of Wonder-Cars made certain claims regarding reliability and finish. It is likely that these claims will be regarded as mere sales talk and will not be terms of the contract. However there is a possibility that by using section 56 of the C.C.A. which states that in any antecedent negotiations (as here where Alan discussed his purchase) then the supplier (Grasping Finance) is directly liable for any misrepresentations made by the credit-broker (Wonder-Cars). Clearly depending on what was actually said, then a misrepresentation action could be considered.

The transaction concerned is one of hire purchase. There would appear to be a breach of condition of section 10 of 1973 Supply of Goods (Implied) Terms Act. This would entitle Alan to reject the goods, recover any monies paid and liability for future instalments would cease. In hire purchase transactions there is no doctrine of acceptance, only affirmation: (*Yeoman* v. *Credit* v. *Apps* 1962; *Shine* v. *General Guarantee* 1988). Affirmation is a question of fact, but on the grounds Alan has constantly complained about the car then he would not appear to have affirmed the contract (*Rogers* v. *Parish* 1986), unlike *Shine* v. *General Guarantee*. Alan should immediately notify the Finance Company telling them he is rejecting the car.

b) Alan purchased the car under a regulated C.C.A. agreement.

This is because it is a hire purchase agreement of credit of less than £15,000 extended to an individual and is not exempt. If there are no faults with the car, and no possibility of cancellation of withdrawal then the only way out for Alan is to terminate the agreement. Under sections 99 and 100 of the C.C.A., where there is a regulated hire purchase agreement (as here) Alan can terminate it as follows:

(a) He is liable for any arrears accrued due ie £900 (£300 per month instalments)

(b) He is liable to bring the payments up to $\frac{1}{2}$ the total price ie £6,400 less £2,000 less £2,700 paid, *i.e.* £1,700 (including arrears). The court has no discretion regarding the arrears but could award a lesser sum than the remaining £800 (unlikely here).

Therefore, if Alan wishes to terminate it is a costly option and he has to hand back the goods.

If he wishes to keep the car as he has already paid more than one third, the goods are protected and cannot be seized back without a court order (C.C.A., s.90). It might be in Alan's best interest to re-negotiate the instalment payments paying only what he can afford, or wait until a default notice is served under Consumer Credit Act, s.87 and then apply for a time order (C.C.A., s.129). This gives a debtor more time to pay, and as it is a hire purchase agreement the order can relate not only to arrears but also to future instalments. The answer therefore depends on whether Alan wishes to keep the car or to return it.

Question 2

John seeks your advice in the following situation.

A week ago he decided to change his car. He went along to his usual garage, Wrecks Motors, where he saw a beautiful sports car. The proprietor, Mr. Smith, told him it was a very economical car, fun and in excellent condition.

John decided to buy it on Hire Purchase. The cash price was £4,700 and Mr. Smith allowed John £1,800 for his old car. John drove the sports car away and told the salesman to send all the necessary forms round to his office to sign.

The following day a salesman came round to the office, where John signed the H.P. forms with Royal Finance Ltd. The total H.P. price, including interest and life insurance premiums (which the Finance Company insisted John take out for three years) was £5,400, the car acting as deposit, leaving a balance of £3,600 to be paid by 36 monthly instalments of £100. John was given a copy of the agreement.

Unfortunately, John's wife detests the car: she took it out for a drive and, being unaccustomed to handling it, scraped it when trying to drive it into the garage. She then declared that she would never drive it again and John must return the car. The damage will cost approximately £100 to put right.

John wants to know whether there is any way he can get out of the agreement without it costing him too much.

Answer

The agreement between John and Royal Finance is a regulated consumer credit agreement under the C.C.A. 1974, being an agreement between an individual and a creditor who provides him with credit not exceeding £15,000 (s.8.). It is not exempt. There is nothing to suggest that John's business is a company. It is a two party restricted use debtor-creditor-supplier agreement as it is H.P. (s.12(a)).

It is not clear from the facts whether the agreement became executed when John signed it. It would be executed if the salesman signed on the "occasion" (s.63(1)). If it was unexecuted there is a possibility that John could withdraw from the prospective agreement. However, notice of withdrawal must reach the other party before acceptance and, as acceptance is valid on posting, Royal Finance Ltd.'s acceptance might already be in the post by the time John's withdrawal arrives. (However, if John purported to withdraw but was too late it would be taken as notice of his cancellation in writing.)

It is a cancellable agreement under section 67 of the C.C.A. 1974 because there were antecedent negotiations involving oral representations in the presence of the debtor (*i.e.* Smith was a credit-broker conducting negotiations in relation to goods to be sold to the debtor within *section 56(1)* and he made statements *re* the car) and the agreement was signed away from business premises of the creditor or negotiator. The agreement can therefore be cancelled by John serving notice of cancellation by the end of the fifth day following the day he receives his second copy or notice of cancellation rights (s.68). If the agreement was unexecuted John must be sent a copy of the executed agreement within seven days of making the agreement (*i.e.* acceptance). If it was executed he must be sent a notice of his cancellation rights within seven days of the agreement being made (s.64).

As it is only six days since he signed and as either a second copy or notice must be sent by post in the case of a cancellable agreement (ss.63(3) and 64(1)(b)) he should be entitled to cancel in either case.

John may cancel by serving a notice in writing on either Wrecks Motors or Royal Finance (s.69(1)) as Wrecks Motors are agents of Royal Finance for this purpose. If he posts the notice it need only be posted by the fifth day. It does not matter whether it arrives at all provided John can prove he posted it in time. The effect of cancellation is to cancel the agreement and any linked transaction (s.69(1)). Although the insurance is a linked transaction within section 19, being in compliance with a term of the principal agreement, it is exempt from the cancellation provisions under the Consumer Credit (Linked Transactions) (Exemptions) Regulations 1983. Therefore John will have to cancel the insurance policy separately. On cancellation the car which was taken in part-exchange must be returned within 10 days of cancellation or the negotiator (Smith) must re-pay the part-exchange allowance of £1,800 to John (s.73). (Although any sum paid by John must also be repaid by the creditor, there is no evidence that John made any payment.) John is under a duty to restore the new car to the other party but need not deliver the goods (s.72), *i.e.* they must collect it. However, he will have a lien over the car for the part-exchange goods/allowance.

Throughout the pre-cancellation period John is under a duty to take reasonable care of the car (C.C.A., s.72(3) 1974) and therefore will have to recompense Royal Finance for the damage done to the car by his wife. For 21 days following cancellation John will still be under this duty (Consumer Credit Act 1974, s.72(8)).

Therefore on the facts John can get out of the agreement by cancelling and it will cost him nothing except for the damage to the car.

John could consider termination but it would be an extreme measure considering the disadvantages and totally unnecessary on the facts.

Although Smith made representations regarding the car there is not enough evidence for misrepresentations.

It is always worth checking whether both creditor (Royal Finance) and credit-broker (Wreck Motors/Smith) are licensed, as if either is not the agreement cannot be enforced without a validating order from the Director General of Fair Trading (ss.40 & 149).

Question 3

(a) Eric recently purchased a kettle from Scurrys. The kettle was advertised by the shop as being "100% stainless steel." When his wife Olive used it she suffered an electric shock and dropped the kettle on her new ceramic tiled floor. The kettle was dented, the floor ruined and Olive was quite badly burned necessitating hospital treatment and time off work.

The kettle was marked "Made in Hong Kong especially for Scurrys." On analysis the kettle was shown to be 80 per cent. aluminium, 20 per cent. stainless steel.

(b) He also purchased with cash a hi-fi system for £120 from "Bargains," a second-hand store. Eric had bought many items there over the years. The shop assistant had said and a clause on the till receipt read "all goods sold as seen; no refunds given under any circumstances." When Eric arrived home with the hi-fi system, he discovered that it would not work at all.

Advise Eric on all his remedies under the civil and criminal law.

Answer

(a) When Eric purchased the kettle from Scurrys his consumer transaction was governed by the 1979 Sale of Goods Act. However the major bulk of any claim is going to be the injuries suffered by Olive who is not a party to the contract. Arguments can be put forward for attempting to make her a party (*Jackson* v. *Horizon Holidays* 1975), but as this could prove difficult the way forward would be to use the 1987 Consumer Protection Act. This Act, introduced as a result of a European Directive, regulates the law on defective products and creates strict liability so far as:

(a) a manufacturer of goods is concerned;
(b) an own brander; or
(c) the first importer into the European Community.

The Act applies in respect of goods supplied after March 1, 1988 and the word "supplies" relates to the time the manufacturer supplied the goods to the retailer. Here it would seem the time limits are satisfied although of course checks would have to be made on this. Primary liability is cast upon the three people outlined above. Obviously Scurrys are not a manufacturer but they could be classed as an own brander (who has held himself out as a producer). Judicial guidance is needed as to whether the words made especially for Scurrys mean that Scurrys are not holding themselves as a producer, at the moment some commentators feel that merely saying that made especially for will not allow own branders to escape liability. In any event Scurrys will be liable as the first importer into the

European Community. The Act imposes strict liability for damage caused by a defective product. This includes any personal injury damage and damage to private property totalling more than £275. There is no compensation under the Act for damage to the product itself (s.5) so nothing can be claimed for the kettle, this would have to be obtained by Eric using the Sale of Goods Act. As the kitchen is private property, provided the damage totals more than £275 then this can be claimed under the Act.

As to the kettle not matching its description, there is an implied condition under section 13 of the Sale of Goods Act 1979 that the goods will correspond with their description. There has obviously been a breach of description, and as reliance was placed on it by Eric there can be no doubt it formed part of the description (*Harlingden and Leinster* v. *Christopher Hull Fine Art* 1991). Eric is therefore entitled to reject the kettle subject to the doctrine of acceptance. Acceptance by keeping the goods beyond a reasonable period of time (*Bernstein* v. *Pamson Motors* 1986) means that the condition in section 13 is reduced to a warranty (Sale of Goods Act, s.11(4)), for which damages only are payable.

As the sellers were acting in the course of a business, as the goods were falsely described, an offence may have been committed under section 1 of the 1968 Trade Descriptions Act. Clearly there has been a false trade description and section 1 creates a strict liability offence subject only to defences set out in section 24 of the Act.

(b) The transaction here is covered by the Sale of Goods Act 1979. By section 14 of the Sale of Goods Act there is an implied condition that where the goods are sold in the course of a business they will be of merchantable quality (as defined by section 14(6)) and will be reasonably fit for their purpose. These conditions also apply to the sale of second-hand goods made in the course of a business, although the price paid is a very relevant factor in deciding whether or not the goods are of merchantable quality (*Bartlett* v. *Sidney Marcus* 1965). Here, as the hi-fi system does not work at all there would appear to be a breach of both conditions thereby entitling Eric to reject the system and get his money back. As this is a non-severable contract, if acceptance has occurred then by section 11(4) of the Sale of Goods Act, the condition becomes a warranty for which damages only are payable. Here, as Eric is returning the goods immediately there can be no question of acceptance. The notice on the till and on the receipt are exclusion clauses.

The first point to be considered is whether or not by the common law rules the clauses have been incorporated in the contract. Assuming their prominent position, incorporation appears to have taken place, and the clauses are therefore governed by the U.C.T.A. The clause is trying to exclude liability for section 14 of the Sale of Goods Act. The effect of the U.C.T.A., s.6 is that any clause which purports to do this is void where the buyer is dealing as a consumer. Is Eric dealing as a consumer? By section 6 of the U.C.T.A. a person deals as a consumer where he buys from someone acting in the course of a business (*i.e.* Bargains), he does not hold himself out as acting in the course of a business, i.e. (Eric is a private buyer) and the goods are normal consumer goods. Eric is therefore dealing as a consumer, the clause is void and Eric is entitled to reject the goods and recover his money.

In addition, by virtue of the 1976 Consumer Transactions (Restrictions on Statement) Order, a trader can be guilty of a criminal offence where he exhibits a void exclusion clause in a notice or till receipt. Bargains could therefore be guilty of a criminal offence.

INDEX